Faith in High Places

To The Presbyterian Church of Timnath

the inspiration for this book

FAITH
IN HIGH
PLACES

Historic Country Churches
of Colorado

JEAN GOODWIN MESSINGER
and
MARY JANE MASSEY RUST
Photography by Mary Jane Massey Rust

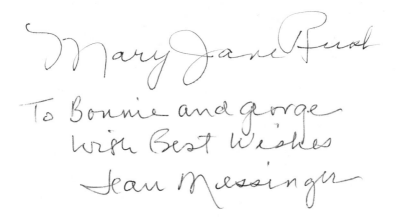

Mary Jane Rust

*To Bonnie and george
with Best Wishes
Jean Messinger*

ROBERTS RINEHART PUBLISHERS

Copyright © 1995 by
Jean Goodwin Messinger and Mary Jane Massey Rust
Published in the United States of America by
Roberts Rinehart Publishers
5455 Spine Road, Mezzanine West
Boulder, Colorado 80301

ISBN 1-57098-013-6
Library of Congress Catalog Card Number 94-74949

Printed in the United States of America
Distributed in the United States and Canada by
Publishers Group West

CONTENTS

Color plates follow page 18

PREFACE

The dedication page of this book may come as a surprise; books are usually dedicated to people. However, it was obvious to us that the Presbyterian Church in Timnath was the most appropriate recipient of that honor. We discovered the church by accident while driving through Timnath. One look at this church and its beautiful windows suggested it was a special place with special people.

On the spot we were inspired to locate other such jewels around Colorado, photograph and research them for publication in book form—soon. One reason for urgency was that small, old churches, precious as they may be, remain a fragile commodity. They burn, their steeples are blown down, and sometimes there isn't enough money to keep both the roof and leaded windows in good repair. Worse yet, until not many years ago they were readily torn down so that new, bigger structures could be built on the same close-to-the-center-of-town lots.

Fortunately, the public has become more aware of the value of historic resources in general for their role in preserving a community's heritage. Not only emotion but economics have entered the picture, giving protection, even new life, to these endangered structures. For a motorized society, being in the heart of town is no longer a necessity, and a new church can be relocated while a smaller congregation takes over the old building. Adaptive reuse is another alternative—practical and quite chic at the moment. Church interior spaces are well suited to a number of purposes; several examples are featured separately in this book. Still, five of the subjects that were selected had to be eliminated during the course of the project. In six months two churches burned, two closed their doors and now face an uncertain future, and one went down in a tornado.

Locating and identifying churches while they are intact was only part of this effort. Photographing a church rarely permits simply standing in the street in front of the building, dodging traffic. Space is required to include some sky above the cross on the tip of the steeple. But the real challenge was literally in the form of obstacles. We wondered if there was a conspiracy to place signs, electric wires, telephone poles, mammoth overgrown conifers, street lights, parked cars, and road repair barricades in front of each church, not to mention maintenance crews, painters and window washers, who seemed to show up on the very day we were there to shoot. These restrictions explain some of the unconventional angles of certain photographs—necessary compromises of a photographer's craft. As for weather, the constant, brilliant blue Colorado sky makes the photographs look like most were taken on the same day. On one occasion, however, we had to rush the work in Las Animas because a tornado was approaching.

Neither of us was prepared for the number, variety, and aesthetic quality of Colorado churches. We discovered architectural treasures in places with names many Coloradans have never heard of. There were so many good subjects that final selection for the book was extremely difficult, even painful. Readers will notice that some denominations, particularly Mormons and Lutherans, are not so well represented in the collection, and that is because their many lovely churches statewide are generally too new for our purpose.

For practicality, the focus of this project was exteriors; few interiors have been included, therefore. The interiors of churches visited match the charm, individuality, and beauty of their exteriors and reflect the same pride. To fully appreciate what a church is all about requires actually going inside, looking around, sitting awhile, listening, and once again looking around. The interior is, after all, the center of a church's heartbeat.

Jean Goodwin Messinger
Mary Jane Massey Rust

ACKNOWLEDGMENTS

We are grateful to the scores of men and women who were literally essential to the production of *Faith in High Places*. All those
rightfully proud keepers of church archives gave us the courage
to pursue a project that could never have come solely from our
two minds, no matter what level of naive enthusiasm we may
have generated between us.

Many thanks to all who responded so enthusiastically to our
inquiries about the histories of their churches, and to those who
said something like, "Say, did you know about the old church
in . . . ?"

Nancy Rust, Gene Smith, Carol Bruce, Barbara Robbins, Fran
Davis, Ann B. Rutledge, Judy Hanell, Lorraine Deppe, Sister Mar-
istelle Schmitz O.S.B., Elizabeth Schroeder, Carol Davis, Pastor
Jim Reid, Alex Ostwald, Donna Miller, Martha Gayler, Doris
Hamilton, Sandy Burton, Janice Herbst, Peggy Lewis, Jane
Basden, Shirley Kasky, Bill and Phyllis Lutz, John Tuttle, Terry
Alixopulis, Priscilla Beshor, Ron Weekes, Father Ted Haas,
Hunter Spence, Ann Ogburn, Wanda Sheets, Zanetta Gregory,
Mr. and Mrs. Virgil Watkins, Mrs. Whitney Miller, Lloyd Glazer,
Mabel Boehm, Betty Harris, Harold Schmidt, Virginia Hinton,
Henry H. "Bud" and Arlene L. Curtis, James Hope, Marilyn
Hasart, Jane Van Dyke, Rose Raab, Dora Jeffers, Gladys Ellerman,
Reverend Warren C. Heintzelman, Jr., Patricia Rust, Rebecca
Fleming, Lori Sanchez.

We depended heavily on local museums, libraries and histori-
cal societies and their staffs. They include: City of Greeley Mu-
seum, Burlington Public Library, Lake County Public Library,
Aspen Historical Society, Buena Vista Heritage Museum, Buena
Vista Chamber of Commerce, Douglas County Public Library
District, Colorado Historical Society, Cortez Public Library, Rio
Grande County Museum and Cultural Center, Eaton Library,
St. Malo Conference Center, South Park City Museum, Fort Mor-
gan Heritage Foundation, Frontier Historical Museum, Mesa
City Public Library, Julesburg Museum, Fort Sedgwick Historical

Society, Elbert County Library, St. Vrain Historical Society, San Luis Cultural Center, Lyons Historical Society, Redstone Museum, Longmont Swedish Society, Alamosa Historical Society, Trinidad Public Library, Colorado Springs Pioneers Museum, Temple Shalom (Colorado Springs), Cripple Creek District Museum.

There were many who went the extra mile tracking down old documents, unpublished papers, newspaper clippings, and early records to add to our growing files: Steve Sorensen, Debbie Strom and the Redstone Inn, Rev. Jon Anderson, Martin and Pauline Nielsen, Norma Oldland, LaVerne M. Johnson, Dale S. Bernard, Pauli Smith, Mary Jenson, Etta Marie Marcy, Gordon J. Hodgin, David Lamb, Father Carl Useldinger, Mrs. Marvin Gardner, Gloria Masterson, Chaplain E. A. Thompson, Della Yersin, Margaret Shellans, Jane Morton, Ruby Henson, Edith Lamb, Joan Lynch, Clara Farmer, Steve and Marlene Hare, Erik Swanson.

Our very special gratitude, appreciation and admiration go to the following experts and friends: Dr. William Holmes, Director of the Pioneers Museum of Colorado Springs, who cheered us on from the very beginning and assured us the project was important. Dale Heckendorn of the Colorado State Historical Society validated the idea of this book, gave us access to state archives and put us in touch with knowledgable source persons. John Sakala, descendant of Czech pioneers, led us on a tour of Orthodox sites around Calhan. He welcomed us to St. Mary's Church with a running commentary on its history as well as the community history of the Czechoslovakian presence in eastern Colorado. Ron Kessler interrupted his day to spend hours recounting Monte Vista and Del Norte stories and took us over the San Luis Valley hardpan to show us preserved ruts from wagons traveling the historic Old Spanish Trail—a surprise bonus! Roger Henn, Ouray historian and expert on George Darley, generously shared with us his great fund of knowledge. Professor Horst Richardson graciously shared with us his research on today's Russian Germans who live along the Volga River.

Thomas Messinger was sometime photographer, sometime chauffeur, and always cheerleader.

Our editor, Toni Knapp, cheerfully kept us from being overwhelmed at the magnitude of this project as it unfolded. The finished book is largely the result of her support, unerring advice, and adroit editing. Thank you, Toni.

PART I
SETTING THE SCENE

ABOUT STYLE

Why Does a Church Look Like a Church?

The post-World War II era saw a great proliferation of church-building activity both in wartorn Europe and in America. These new structures often bear little resemblance to what believers have accepted for several centuries as the proper form and appearance of a Christian house of worship. It takes rethinking to be comfortable with something that departs radically from those expectations. Traditions which developed out of functional and symbolic needs of long ago have become entrenched as though they were sacred prescriptions lifted from the pages of the Scriptures. We think we know by now what a church should look like, and we like a church to look like a church.

In reality, these are times of professional, trained architects working with entirely different considerations. Twentieth-century congregations have no need for a watchtower to warn of barbarian invaders from the north, nor for a bell to summon the militia or announce the commencement of Sunday services to a populace without time-telling devices. Wide, long, side aisles that lead toward and around the altar are not relevant to modern Roman Catholic churches nor to Protestant churches at all. Such aisles were originally intended to facilitate traffic flow on church holidays for medieval pilgrims who came to view saintly relics or other treasures brought back from the Crusades.

These are just a few of the traditional features that identify a structure as a church and not, for example, a hospital—features which we regard with affection while recognizing that they do add to the cost as well as the charm of our favorite landmarks.

Historical Perspectives

Early American builders and designers adopted familiar European styles for their churches as well as for other structures. Sometimes they used designs from standard pattern books, sometimes combining a steeple from one model with windows, front entrance, or some other feature, from another source. Even more undisciplined inspiration was common practice during Victorian times.

Yet, in the New World, certain concerns such as materials availability, scale requirements, and the degree of permanence, were somewhat different from their traditional European counterparts, demonstrating that indeed New World problems asked for New World solutions. For example, in America, building technology brought by the immigrants was applied more to the use of wood and bricks than to stone, because the former were more accessible and more appropriate for Colonial needs. In the desert Southwest, however, adobe bricks provided a practical alternative to scarce wood and stone, resulting in the distinctive adobe style still popular in that part of the United States.

By transplanting the contemporary Georgian architectural style from Britain to the colonies during the eighteenth century, settlers were continuing the use of Classical motifs from ancient Greece and Rome via the Renaissance by applying them to their own, new churches. Models for the white steeple church commonly associated with the eastern seaboard originated in England in the eighteenth-century work of James Gibbs, architect of London's St. Martin's in the Field. That form is still the Christmas card stereotype of an American church, and its variations can be found throughout the United States. Perhaps some Americans of the eighteenth and nineteenth centuries had forgotten or were unaware that Classical temples were once considered sacreligious inspiration for Christian houses of worship. During the Counter Reformation in the sixteenth century, the Roman Catholic church objected to allowing Christian worship in space that looked like a temple for pagan Greeks and Romans of the ancient world. The opposition was directed more toward what such a structure symbolized than its artistic form.

Otherwise, architects and patrons of the Italian Renaissance beginning in the early fifteenth century were quite taken by the beauty of Classical architecture. They responded to its symmetry, perfect proportions, graceful white columns, imposing domes, and elegant, simple decoration. As Christians, these same architects and patrons accepted the Classical style for their own churches. Thus literal translations of the Pantheon in Rome are alive and well in more than one Colorado community.

Subsequent embellishment of the original pure Classical style produced excesses to be sure, but in essence the expanded design system developed during the Renaissance has hardly been out of style for nearly 500 years. Throughout Colorado, in mountain communities, Front Range cities, and rural railroad towns of the eastern plains, Classical references are visible today on all categories of monumental buildings, including churches. No matter how grand, no matter how spare, the effect remains one of repose, clarity, and dignity. Even as these characteristics appear on Colorado churches, they are consistent with the ideals proposed by the ancients—human ideals that are not so incompatible with the beliefs these churches represent.

But neither Americans nor Coloradans designed all their churches from the same inspiration. As the frontier moved westward, the nineteenth century was introduced to another major religious revival style. By the time Charles Darwin's theories were shaking up mid-Victorian certitudes, British designers of churches had for several years been looking back to the Middle Ages for theologically honest prototypes. This time the models were thoroughly Christian. Back in the thirteenth and fourteenth centuries, builders of cathedrals emphasized vertical lines; their approach to design reflected preoccupation with things of the spirit. The reach toward heaven can be seen in their tall towers, vast interior spatial heights, and pointed arches. Stone walls were punctured by numerous windows, some large enough to require reinforcing stone tracery to ensure structural strength. Irregularity and asymmetry were often the result of several centuries separating their construction, but Victorian revivalists capitalized on such freedom and applied it flamboyantly.

The Gothic Revival originated from a philosophy and design

system in opposition to Classicism of the ancient world, and once again the latter was unjustly defamed for what it was not even attempting to be. In contrast to Gothic style, Classical design was unified and very harmonious. Every element contributed and was essential to the sum; removal of one part destroyed the integrity of the whole. Ancient designers emphasized horizontality in order to express stability, permanence, and solidity—goals quite different from those of medieval cathedral builders.

On the American frontier, which was getting farther and farther away from the rule books of the eastern United States and England, builders took advantage of their choices. The pretentious and less secure among them tried hard to project an image of propriety and sophistication by reproducing that which was admired back east. Others created their own standards. In addition, many buildings throughout America as well as several Colorado churches under discussion here were designed and built by people who didn't know there were rules—neither historical nor philosophical associations were of concern to them. Consequently, it was common practice for such builders to combine design and structural elements from here and there without regard for consistency, appropriateness, or origin of style. However, the naiveté and sincerity of such an approach often produced a surprisingly pleasing result.

The resulting polystyle made labeling difficult, and so the term *eclectic* was applied to identify and describe these situations; mixing lineage was a practice savored by the Victorians. An eclectic structure can be a bizarre mishmash, or it can be charming and aesthetically successful. Always it will be unique, and in America we do claim to prize individuality.

Vernacular is another term which can be applied to certain Colorado churches. It roughly refers to folk forms: barns, country bridges, log cabins, country schoolhouses, small churches, and farmhouses—structures built without architects, from indigenous materials, and according to local or personal circumstances. Whether textbook revival, eclectic, vernacular or original, American places of worship are often as different from each other as they are from Norwegian stave churches and Iranian mosques. Their design inspiration comes from a variety of sources.

In the range of social structures the public builds for itself, none is as personal and as expressive as religious spaces are in America. Perhaps this can be explained best by understanding the close relationships individuals and families often have with their church—relationships that can continue for many generations. Worshipers also have a proprietary interest in the structure itself, and therefore a measure of control and responsibility for the success of its mission. The degree of commitment is obvious in the love and pride displayed by careful maintenance of the premises. All this is very evident in the examples appearing on the pages following, but it is fair to say that throughout the state, we found very few neglected-looking churches in use.

It is likely that this love affair with churches contributes to the stylistic uniqueness of each one and to what could be described as "personality." Although it is helpful to understand why things are the way they are and appreciate their variety, categorizing and stylistic analysis are not the focus of this book. Shakespeare told us long ago that names don't matter much. Yogi Berra might just put it this way—*it is what it is.*

BEGINNINGS

ifferent sections of Colorado were settled at different times and for various purposes by people who entered the territory or state under a wide range of circumstances. For example, the San Luis Valley in southern Colorado was at one time part of the New Mexico Territory and originally part of Mexico, which had been conquered in the sixteenth century by Spaniards under the Spanish Crown. As such, the valley was an extension of the Hispanic culture and was penetrated earlier than the rest of Colorado. It also meant settlers were predominately Catholic, continuing a 300-year-old tradition in the American Southwest.

Eastern prospectors who came to the mountains during the 1850s and 1860s were not settlers *per se,* and religion was not their game. Mining camps required some civilizing before they became appropriate for families, much less for churches. Getting the goldseekers—a category that included gambling-hall proprietors, saloon-keepers, and prostitutes—to their knees was always a challenge for the circuit-riding preachers. On the other hand, agricultural settlements of the eastern plains, front range, and parts of the western slope did attract families, many of whom came from a church-going tradition back east or in Europe. They brought Sunday with them in a multitude of affiliations, and each preferred its own worship space. Some settlements were initiated by immigrants of a single sect.

Once believers found themselves among friends, so to speak, they gathered for prayer meetings and held services, often without a preacher or priest. With characteristic pioneer resourcefulness they worshiped wherever there was space or shelter. They sometimes met in each other's cabins and homes, as some early congregations consisted of fewer than a dozen individuals. In 1872, Fort Collins Presbyterians held their organizational meeting with the celebrated missionary Reverend Sheldon Jackson under cottonwoods along the Cache la Poudre River.

Any interior space large enough for assembly served multiple purposes on the frontier. What might be designated officially as the courthouse, school, town hall, or church likely was used for a combination of those functions during the course of the week. In the booming mining centers such as Leadville, there were occasions when dance halls, saloons, gambling dens, and the general store were called upon to provide space, even an audience, for hearing the Word when the circuit rider came to town. Since his arrival was infrequent, business was not disrupted too seriously. In fact, it was often the proprietor himself who called out, "O.K., boys, put away the cards!" announcing that all activity would be suspended in order for patrons to give the preacher an opportunity to cleanse their souls. At the gaming tables, winners were more willing than losers, but it was hard for anyone to resist the rather forceful passing of the hat—a gesture which contributed to salvation for preacher and miners alike.

Church headquarters back east seemed to regard their Western missions in terms of competition for virgin frontier markets. Protestants and Catholics, of course, had rivalries going back centuries. Protestants in America felt particularly threatened by Roman Catholic expansion into Western territories, where Catholics already had an advantage from Spanish colonialism. Nevertheless, in Colorado, Protestants also raced against each other, and Lutherans made accusations of encroachment against other Lutherans. On the other hand, missionaries and immigrants themselves were more relaxed about affiliations, and logistics blurred denominational loyalties. Whoever got to a given locality first with a missionary people liked, had a head start establishing a church. With scant material resources and limited numbers of sympathetic worshipers, cooperative effort was beneficial and at times essential.

The first structure actually built as a church in a given community might be built by one denomination who shared it with the others until they could each build their own. On Sundays they took turns, scheduling their respective services at different times throughout the day. Or the building itself might be a collective venture from the beginning and serve as a community church with all denominations attending the same service. That was a practical solution which still works today in many small Colorado towns.

Some town councils and colony promoters donated land for churches, recognizing that the actual appearance of a church structure would give the impression of a settlement's respectability and permanence. The earliest structures were often built by parishioners themselves and depended upon donations for material as well as labor. If a community prospered, its success was reflected in the upscaling of its churches; the original structure was usually torn down. At the same time, wooden churches succumbed easily to fire, inspiring the construction of a more ambitious replacement. As a result of such natural processes, many churches throughout Colorado today are third-generation versions of long-established congregations.

Sometimes disasters were not so natural. In Cortez, according to recollections by Paul Wilson, the Congregational Church was destroyed by a fire caused by "loiterers sleeping in the bell-tower room." Cortez Presbyterians lost their house of worship by misguided intentions of the pastor's son, who had overheard remarks to the effect that "the only way they would get a nice new church was for their building to burn."

As unique as every structure was, each upscaled phase usually acknowledged increasing reference to national styles of the day— styles that were set in the East. There was a great deal of pride involved; folks on the frontier did not want to be seen as backward, unsophisticated or, heaven forbid, stingy. Their monumental structures in general were the very best they could afford, therefore, and in some cases surprisingly grand for the setting and circumstances. Some creditable examples remain, and churches are among the most impressive of these.

In the rural and small-town locations which were the scope of this survey of Colorado churches, subjects are rarely grandiose and only sometimes monumental. However, they are most definitely not short on beauty, charm, and sincerity. They are best described collectively in terms of the recurring themes that are revealed in their stories. Those themes call to mind "people" words that describe the relationship between churches and their people—words such as resilience, sacrifice, resourcefulness, dedication, pride and, oh yes—faith.

TRAILBLAZERS

ven the most romantic perceptions of the Wild West fail to acknowledge the role of certain heroes who were on the side of a higher sort of Law. Colorado history books make little mention of its early missionaries, who often risked their lives just getting from one camp or settlement to the next. Although no tunnels or counties and only a few mountain peaks immortalize their names, they, too, helped tame and build the West. Their influence was significant and enduring.

In the Hispanic southern portion of Colorado Territory, under Bishop Lamy of Santa Fe, Catholic settlers continued to feel the protective, connecting arm of their faith. Elsewhere, even before there were settlements, there was a role for chaplains at army posts. Mining camps and isolated farms and villages of the rest of Colorado faced different challenges, however. Protestant missionary districts were organized and administered from the East by well-meaning authorities who had little conception of the obstacles or the culture shock that awaited their emissaries.

The Reverend A. T. Rankin, one of the first Presbyterian ministers to come to Colorado, left a detailed diary of his impressions. He was shocked by the capricious murder he witnessed on the streets of Denver in 1860 and disturbed by wanton sport shooting of buffalo by stagecoach passengers. Rankin and other Eastern preachers were equally horrified by the disrespect shown for the Sabbath. In a general sense, proselytizing of the West was aimed at preventing social anarchy and moral breakdown, which the Eastern establishment feared would result from the free and lawless conditions existing on the frontier. However, retaining denominational membership as well as salvation of souls motivated home mission activity.

Missionary districts were enormous, initially composed of several territories or states. The Episcopal Northwest District was established in 1859 and consisted of eight present-day Western states. Its bishop, Joseph Talbott, referred to himself as "bishop of all outdoors." Sheldon Jackson was appointed Superintendent of Missions of the Rocky Mountain Region, an unmanageable domain that originally included western Iowa, Nebraska, North and South Dakota, Wyoming, Montana, Utah, and later Colorado, New Mexico, and Arizona!

Missionaries were also separated by hundreds of miles from all practical contact with their eastern bases. When John Kehler established Episcopal St. John's in the Wilderness in Denver in 1860, the nearest other Episcopalian church was in Topeka—700 miles away. Reverend Horace Hitchings living in Connecticut had never heard of Denver or Colorado when he received his call to St. John's in 1862, nor could he locate either on a map. Then there is the oft-told story about the eminent Episcopalian bishop, George Maxwell Randall. Upon being assigned to Wyoming Territory in 1865, he wrote from Denver to his superiors back east, "After diligent inquiry and research I have not been able to discover any such territory. . . ." Present-day Wyoming may not be so obscure, but many of the settlements served by early circuit riders no longer exist and would not be found on a current map.

A single railroad line linked the two coasts in 1869, and long-distance transport within the Colorado Territory still depended largely on horse power. The great distances from one station to another were covered on foot or on horseback in all kinds of weather, usually solo over primitive trails. The mountain circuit riders expected to encounter wolves, bears, hostile Indians, ill effects from the high altitude, and waist-deep snow. They often slept on the ground under a buffalo robe. It was not uncommon to cross the mountains at night when the snow was crusted, which made walking easier. The Reverend Lewis Hamilton, first Presbyterian minister in Colorado, did so at age 70.

Before the days of Gortex, freeze-dried stew and energy bars, and helicopter rescue, it was nevertheless a time when a stranger would receive hospitality when he found a cabin, and the preacher was always welcomed. In a letter written in 1878, the Catholic Father Joseph Machebeuf described traveling in his buggy 300 miles from Lake City to Denver over dangerous roads and bridges with every step requiring caution. Coming down an incline, the horses stumbled, ". . . crowding them to the edge of the precipice and pitching us over upon the rocks. . . . Through the protection of the Archangel Raphael, whose Mass I had said that morning, I escaped with only a few scratches. . . . The top of the buggy was broken into a thousand pieces. It happened in sight of a house of a good German . . ." who not only rescued the priest and his party but had the buggy repaired at his own expense and transported Father Machebeuf on his rounds in the meantime.

On the eastern prairies, conditions were somewhat different. Footing was easier and there was no altitude sickness, but there were still unfriendly Indians plus rattlesnakes, high winds on a barren landscape, electrical storms, and lack of water. No matter what the destination, route, or mode used to get there, the circuit rider was equally challenged by the dangers and discomforts of solitude.

Even in good company there were hazards. Father Machebeuf was robbed while riding the stage over Mosquito Pass. In addition, there were perils unimaginable in the twentieth century; Father Machebeuf described one: ". . . the smallpox was raging, especially among the children of the Mexicans, and my boy-driver and I had often to eat and sleep in the very room where three or four were sick, and it might be one or two dead, but we never had the slightest symptoms of the disease." His faith in Archangel Raphael need not be questioned.

In the early days, visits from a preacher were infrequent. A wedding or baptism could wait, but a burial could not. In between visits, those who were accustomed to devotional activities arranged their own Bible-reading, singing, and fellowship. Hymnals were rarer than Bibles, but good memories and strong voices compensated, sometimes accompanied by a melodeon.

No matter what his skills or spiritual equipment, the missionary played an important social role as well. His profession had a certain charisma, as the preacher was a contact with the outside world, a representative of civilization no matter how scruffy he looked when he arrived. His presence gave sanction and encouragement to a new congregation and to the life passages that were important to its members. He also stood for something to the nonbeliever and unaffiliated—he was a man to be trusted, and they respected his courage.

The physical and psychological drain on these tough spiritual trailblazers took its toll. Some had to leave their assignments early because they were unsuited to frontier ministry and/or their health failed. The emotional stress alone tested the limits of the strongest heart: anguish from attempting to console in times of illness in those days when medical technology was so inaccessible; frequent burial of babies, children, and young mothers; and for all ages the ever-present mortal dangers of the environment—rattlesnake bites, avalanches, mine cave-ins, and life-threatening weather conditions. The transient nature of the population made lack of commitment another frustration for the preacher. The missionary Reverend Cyrus Townsend Brady wrote in his memoirs that his job was the most "exhausting, wearying, heartbreaking lot that can fall to any mortal man."

Brady could have added "poorly paid," as the preacher depended largely on his own success at collecting donations, which was often tied to how effectively he got his message across. Given the circumstances under which he sometimes had to preach, these were always uncertainties. It was not uncommon for miners to shake gold dust into the collection plate. Indifferent listeners or devoted flock, they usually didn't have much to share anyway. Even established churches had a hard time compensating the preacher. During "pound days" at harvest time, parishioners donated a pound of items like sugar, flour, corn, or molasses to help feed the preacher's family. Apparently something other than remuneration was the motivation for the extraordinary dedication of these larger-than-life pioneers who brought the Faith to Colorado.

Bishop Joseph Machebeuf

The earliest of Colorado's legendary missionary evangelists was French-born Joseph Machebeuf, who became bishop of Colorado and Utah in 1868 and later bishop of Denver. He was a boyhood friend of the eminent bishop of Santa Fe, Jean Baptiste Lamy, the subject of Willa Cather's novel *Death Comes for the Archbishop*. After Lamy was named bishop in 1850 at the end of the Mexican War, he sent for Machebeuf, his old friend and former associate, and made him his vicar general. The two had already served together in the mission fields of the Great Lakes region and continued that effort in the newly-acquired territories of New Mexico and Arizona.

Although Machebeuf was small and frail and no longer a young man, his superior was confident that he was the right man to send north in 1860 to the Colorado gold fields. No one had a clear idea of the challenges Father Machebeuf would face in that vast, unfamiliar land which included eastern plains, mountains, and the San Luis Valley. Many other itinerants walked or rode horseback, but Father Machebeuf relied on a horse-drawn wagon or buggy, which not only carried his vestments and ritual requirements but served as living quarters on the road—the original RV. From his record of mishaps it would seem that he was accident-prone, but in the context of the precarious circumstances he faced in his daily life, perhaps he was blessed with good fortune. He did survive them all.

Father Machebeuf was very much a priest of the people and a consistent advocate for his flock. He is affectionately remembered as the "Apostle of Colorado." Machebeuf's name is attached in some way to many of the Catholic churches represented in this book. He died in Denver in 1889. The substantial growth and accomplishments of Colorado's Roman Catholic community during the years of his service were inspired by his personal leadership.

The Episcopalians

The Episcopal church in Colorado claims a number of outstanding frontier churchmen. The bishops in particular left detailed journals, letters, and formal reports which described their reactions to the unexpected circumstances and working conditions they encountered in the field. To be sure, theirs was a ministry unimagined by their colleagues back east.

John Kehler was a 62-year-old widower from Sharpsburg, Mary-
land, and father of 11 children when he came west as a missionary
to the Cherry Creek gold camps in 1860. His portrait shows a man
with shoulder-length hair and a strong, granite face that would in-
spire total confidence that he could handle any challenge. Two
years later, after establishing St. John's in the Wilderness in
Denver, he signed on as chaplain with Colorado's First Regiment,
resigned from his pastorate, and donned a Union Army uniform.
(That regiment achieved fame earlier in the Civil War Battle of
Glorieta Pass in New Mexico, under the leadership of Major John
Chivington of Sand Creek Massacre notoriety. Ironically, Chivington was a Methodist minister when he wasn't soldiering.)

Right Reverend James Maxwell Randall, a New Englander, was
elected first missionary bishop of Colorado "and parts adjacent"
in 1865 and came west the following year. Even though he
couldn't find Wyoming he was a dauntless traveler, a businessman with vision, and determined builder of churches and schools.
He preached, orated, organized, and raised money like no one
else, during a relatively short career in Colorado. Bishop Randall
not only had an exhausting itinerary in his multi-territory district, but he also traveled throughout the East trying to raise
money for his frontier missions. Other denominations had the
same dependency upon outside funding, and the role of Eastern
support should not be minimized. Those who gave responded
generously with endowments, sponsorship of salaries and gifts of
cash, plus church bells, organs, stained-glass windows, and supplies. Still, there was never enough, no matter who was in charge.

Bishop Randall was a gentle and dignified man although extremely ambitious for his cause. He is described as indulging in
one excess—work. But if he had a specific passion it was establishing educational institutions in Colorado. He started schools
for girls, for boys, for theological training, and one in Golden
that later became the Colorado School of Mines.

His death in 1873 was attributed to "typhoid pneumonia" that
resulted from exposure suffered on a particularly arduous trip to
minister to Shoshones on the Wind River Reservation in Wyoming. In death he may have gotten his wish to "wear out rather
than rust out," but at 64 he was still a vigorous and active man.

Fortunately for Colorado and for the struggling Episcopalian Missionary District, an apt successor was chosen to assume the gargantuan tasks of Bishop Randall. With optimism and capabilities to match his substantial size, John Franklin Spaulding was dropped into the cauldron of Western affairs from Erie, Pennsylvania. For the most part, Bishop Spaulding concentrated his activities in the urban areas, particularly Denver. His dream, the new Cathedral of St. John's, was begun in 1880. The 28 years of his episcopate was a period of statewide expansion of the church, and Bishop Spaulding is acknowledged as among the empire builders of the West.

Sheldon Jackson

The name that dominates Presbyterian expansion into Colorado is Sheldon Jackson. Jackson was a man of remarkable energy and conviction who seemed born to proselytize. His task on the Western frontier required superhuman effort and certainly public relations expertise. He was in fact a skilled publicist and fundraiser; his efforts in the West were primarily directed toward organizing rather than to matters of theology.

Sheldon Jackson was from New York State, attended Union College in Schenectady, and graduated from Princeton Seminary in 1858. After brief missionary activities with Choctaw Indians in Oklahoma and ten more years in Minnesota, he came to Denver in 1870 to supervise mission activity in a multi-state area. Subsequently his field was reduced to more manageable and realistic boundaries, and he was able to concentrate on Colorado's needs. As he traveled the state organizing congregations, he reported his experiences in much the same terms of hardship and challenge as his contemporaries did. Although his tactics and style were sometimes controversial, many existing Presbyterian churches proudly claim their origins as "Jackson" churches.

After he left Denver in 1881, the intrepid Jackson went to Alaska and attained new distinction there in education. He was Superintendent of Public Instruction from 1885 to 1908 and started a college in Sitka. He died in 1909 in Asheville, North Carolina.

St. Thomas Episcopal, Alamosa. Unexpected application of adobe styling.

The stereotypical American church, as exemplified in the Church of Christ, Berthoud. J. Messinger photo.

Pantheon on the plains: First Presbyterian in Sterling.

Note classical details of the First Church of Christ Scientist in Glenwood Springs.

The abandoned Church of Christ Scientist in Victor emulated the classical look.

The First Congregational Church in Ault reaches heavenward like its medieval predecessors.

Christ Episcopal, Canon City. Stone tracery stabilizes cathedral-type window.

The Old Church (formerly First Presbyterian) in Leadville features eccentric roof treatment.

The Classical design of First Baptist Church in Greeley. Simple, dignified—and pagan.

Vernacular style as exemplified by Ward Congregational in Ward, which dates from around 1894.

First Christian Church in Manzanola, well-maintained with love and pride.

St. Agnes Catholic Church in Saguache—one of a kind.

Crested Butte's Union Congregational Church in the dawn's early light.

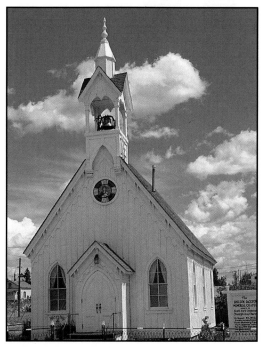

Fairplay Community Church.

Only in Colorado: Father Dyer United Methodist Church in Breckenridge, show-ing Dyer on skis.

John Lewis (Father) Dyer

In the dome of the state capitol building in Denver are 16 stained-glass portraits of outstanding Coloradans. Only one of these is a churchman, the beloved "snowshoe itinerant" known as Father Dyer. He is remembered mostly for his associations with South Park, but during his active missionary years his work took him to locations throughout much of Colorado and into New Mexico. The most imaginative fiction writer could not concoct episodes to match the real-life ordeals of this courageous man.

Born in 1812, John Lewis Dyer had a fundamentalist Methodist upbringing in Ohio and Illinois and little formal education. He married in 1833, and a decade later settled in southwest Wisconsin where he worked in the lead mines. His wife died leaving him with five children, one of whom also died soon after. He wrote that this loss almost crushed his spirit; he had no money and "nothing but my hands to depend upon." A hasty second marriage quickly ended in divorce.

He did some amateur preaching, badly he admits, but subsequently improved his speaking enough to devote the next several years to itinerant preaching in Wisconsin and Minnesota. Then in May of 1861, despite suffering serious eye problems, John Dyer headed west for Pikes Peak country on a horse. Near Omaha, the horse sickened and had to be sold. Dyer walked the rest of the way, 600 miles, in the company of a wagon train. When he arrived in Denver on June 20th he was 49 years old. A few days later he set out to walk 100 miles further to South Park in order to save a $10 stage fare. It was a hike he made several times during the following years—he could cover that distance in only two and a half days.

Father Dyer's ministry in the mining camps epitomizes what has already been discussed as typical of the itinerants' travails. Fortunately, John Dyer was a powerfully built man, and he could hold his own against the challenges of nature and against the unruly toughs he sometimes encountered in his travels. However, he describes the impromptu assemblies in tents and saloons as being receptive and attentive. The robust miners seemed to tolerate his persistent railing against their sinful entertainments:

dancing, drinking, gambling, and theatre. The title "Father" was in fact a term of respect and affection applied informally but not indiscriminately to certain preachers of all denominations.

In his autobiography, Father Dyer describes walking from one camp to another, traveling at night during winter because the five-foot snows "wouldn't bear a man in the daytime even with snowshoes . . . and a horse could not go at all." The snowshoes he speaks of were Norwegian-style skis seven to nine feet long, and Father Dyer made his own. His lifestyle was often primitive but his needs were understandably simple; he changed home base so frequently, simplicity was imperative. When hard up for cash, a chronic condition, Father Dyer tried prospecting; and for one winter he carried the mail 36 miles over Mosquito Pass once a week while maintaining his preaching schedule. Loaded down on skis with 25 pounds of mail plus his personal pack, he also carried out gold dust for the miners. The one thing he did not carry was a gun.

The physical hardships and dangers which Father Dyer survived were not unlike those faced by his colleagues, but they were no match for the heartbreak he suffered from additional family tragedies. One son was lost at sea during the Civil War after being released from Andersonville Prison; another son lost a foot in battle. The remaining son, Elias, was Lake County probate judge, assassinated by vigilantes in his own courtroom in Granite in 1875. It was a highly publicized incident at the time, and one of the perpetrators (none were punished) was a man whose life Father Dyer had saved in the mountains some years earlier.

He was laid to rest in 1901 at age 89 and is buried at Cedar Hill Cemetery in Castle Rock alongside Elias and his own father. Just months prior to his death, Father Dyer was able to climb the steps of the capitol to see the memorial window placed there in his honor. In 1980 as part of the centennial celebration of the Father Dyer United Methodist Church in Breckenridge, a ridge in the mountains he knew so well was named "Father Dyer Peak."

Father Dyer recorded his thoughts and experiences modestly in an autobiography entitled *Snowshoe Itinerant* published in 1890. That work was reprinted in 1975 by the Breckenridge church, and it is hearty and inspiring reading. A more thorough accounting of the man and his life was compiled by Reverend Mark Fiester in *Look for Me in Heaven*. The title was inspired by a dramatic incident related by Father Dyer which occurred when he was on one of his winter treks in the mountains. Alone, lost, and half-frozen, he thought he was facing death and prepared to leave that message on a tree for whoever might find him after it was too late.

George Darley

Another highly-regarded ministry was that of George Darley. His long career was served in several state-wide locations and in varying positions of responsibility. After receiving an honorary divinity degree, he was always referred to as Doctor Darley. He had left school at age 14 to follow his Scottish father's carpenter trade. Later, working in Galveston, he began to preach to dock workers and jail inmates. An older brother, Alexander, was already an ordained minister who achieved his own fame establishing Presbyterianism in the San Luis Valley. Alexander was in Del Norte organizing a Presbyterian church when George joined him there.

The structure George Darley built in 1876 was a simple "schoolhouse" rectangle. An 1898 photo shows the tower addition and a pair of windows at its frontal base with a door on either side. It was soon discovered that caskets couldn't make the sharp turn into the sanctuary, so a straight-on entrance replaced the front windows.

The two brothers went to Lake City in 1876 for the same purpose and gathered a small congregation. George remained behind to build the church, and five months later the job was done. This simple but well-built structure is the oldest church on the western slope of the Colorado Rockies. It has been modified, but its pews and pulpit are also the work of George Darley and are still in use. He stayed on as pastor and built the nearby manse two years later to replace the eight-by-ten-foot dirt-floor cabin his family of five was living in. The manse is also still used, modernized but otherwise unchanged.

An episode of this time alerts us to the kind of stuff George Darley was made of. It is his legendary 125-mile journey from

Lake City on a circuitous route over snowbound mountains to
Ouray in March of 1877. The distance was covered in an unbelievable five days; his companions were a young printer and one
burro. In addition to the usual perils of negotiating deep, ava-
lanche-prone spring snow, they were subjected to icy baths while
crossing the Uncompahgre River 21 times. Darley could scarcely
stand when they arrived, and he was unable to preach until several days later—the first sermon preached in Ouray and in the
Uncompahgre region.

During the summer of that same year, 1877, a congregation
was organized in Ouray, and Dr. Darley returned to build their
church. There wasn't much of a town yet—a general store, three
saloons, a butcher shop. . . . In October, he dedicated the new
building but for some reason was not retained as its pastor. Apparently this was a surprise and disappointment to all concerned.
On his way back to Lake City, he was caught in another snow-
storm and made that same arduous trek in waist-deep snow without snowshoes. He modestly dismissed the adventure in his
memoirs, ". . . walking was difficult going into Ouray to preach
the first sermon, and getting out of Ouray after the first church
was dedicated . . . ," complaining only that he had lost a pair of
valued buckskin leggings. (Coincidentally, this same mountain
route near Lake City was the setting for Alferd Packer's infamous
human dinners three years before. When Packer was brought
into court and charged with cannibalism, the judge accused him
of eating five of the county's six Democrats!)

Altitude and exhaustion soon forced George Darley to leave
Lake City. He was reassigned to Del Norte, then to Fort Morgan
and to Denver, all of which were productive ministries. In 1898,
the call finally came to serve the First Presbyterian Church at
Ouray, 21 years after he had built the first church there. His pop-
ularity intact, "Brother" Darley seemed to be everyone's pastor,
and he ministered to all who needed his help. When questioned
about the propriety of some of his associations, he wrote in his
recollections of those days, "If I could not know and . . . 'associate' with all classes, I was not the man for the place." Even so,
Darley was a temperate man who campaigned relentlessly against
drinking and gambling, from the pulpit and from inside the sin-

ners' own territory. His relentless crusade to collect signatures for his "Pledge" campaign resulted in hundreds of signers but no noticeable reduction in saloon patronage, at least none that was admitted. Yet he was big enough to concede that "a more convenient pulpit than a farotable could not be found; nor a more respectful and intelligent audience."

In lionizing this outstanding human being, it is easy to overlook the role of Darley's wife, Emma Jean. She was as beloved as he and noted for her hospitality. The Darley home was open to everyone, and no one was turned away without a meal. At the same time, they had little to share. When a package of donated clothing came from the Mission Board back east, George had to borrow money to pay the freight. When the box was opened they found items donated by wealthy women that were suitable for fancy balls and tea parties. None of it could be used in Lake City by Emma Jean Darley.

Her burden was heavy. With grace, she managed the instability of frequent moves, periods of separation and isolation, worry about her husband's safety, the death of two young daughters, frequent illness, and never enough money—not an uncommon slate for many pioneer women. However, the Darleys' three successful sons were a source of pride—a lawyer, a minister, and a forester. A grandson, Ward, became president of the University of Colorado.

George Darley died in Alamosa in 1917 at age 70, and Emma Jean died the following year.

Each summer a group from Ouray makes a day trip by jeep to commemorate George Darley's historic 1877 trek over Engineer Mountain Pass. They are often joined by members of other churches once served by his ministry. The caravan takes a different, shorter route, one which Darley himself used in later trips between the two towns. How surprised George Darley would be to know that one of those that presented such obstacles to his passage is now called Darley Mountain. And it all started with a 125-mile walk to preach a sermon in Ouray.

PART II
THE CHURCHES

MOUNTAINS

Aspen Community Church

There is no place quite like Aspen, and it hardly fits the image of small-town Colorado. Residents still pay water bills, need a hospital and schools, and go to church, but Aspen is a mecca for incomparable skiing and the site of a world-class music festival. It has come full circle from silver boomtown in the 1890s, to economic decline when mining activity slowed, and reviving as a picturesque ski resort and playground for the rich and famous a century later. It follows that an architectural jewel in the form of a house of worship from its earlier "glory days" would represent the town's resilience as well as its style.

A handsome, red sandstone church stands on a quiet street not far from chic restaurants and boutiques frequented by an international crowd of visitors. Its cornerstone is a reminder that there has been a community here for over 100 years. Built in 1890 by Presbyterians, this building has been the Aspen Community Church since 1934, even providing worship space for Jewish services for several years during the 1980s. The sanctuary contains the original semi-circular pews which seat 350 people, and the original Victorian, stained-glass windows. Peachblow sandstone for the exterior came from the Frying Pan River Valley near Basalt 18 miles away. This important historic building is on the National Register of Historic Places.

The architect of the building is not known, which is regrettable, because the competent reference to Richardsonian Romanesque style suggests that there may have been one. Since the Aspen church and the Lyons Congregational Church are the only examples of this major American style to be featured in this book, it is appropriate to discuss that influence.

Henry Hobson Richardson was born (1838) and raised in

27

Aspen Community Church

Louisiana. He studied engineering at Harvard, then went off to Paris to learn what he considered to be a more romantic profession—architecture. Fortunately, the very academic, Classical-oriented program at the famous Ecole des Beaux Arts didn't cure the romantic in Richardson. The Civil War prevented him from returning home to Louisiana, but at the end of the war he returned and settled in Boston. Richardson attracted national attention for his early Boston masterpiece, Trinity Church (1872–77). That building launched the acceptance of what became known as "Richardsonian Romanesque." Richardson died in 1886 at age 47, and the style he created remained popular into the 1890s. Richardson is credited with being the first of the three giants who transformed American architecture (Richardson, Louis Sullivan, and Frank Lloyd Wright).

Aspen Community Church bears several Richardsonian characteristics. For example, the exterior is rough-cut ashlar, which in Colorado is often red sandstone. Windows are deep-set and organized in groups, not the tall or large single windows commonly seen on Gothic-like churches. The massive round tower and cross gables are typical, and there is a feeling of solid mass about the structure. The magnificent round arch with its radiating voussoirs and carved foliated detail is Richardson's signature.

The Aspen church is neither ostentatious nor pretentious, but it does bespeak the affluence of its beginnings and probably a conservative element within that. At any rate, it has outlasted most of its neighbors, although its cornerstone was the first real cornerstone laid in Aspen. One other brush with greatness concerns its organ. Albert Schweitzer visited the United States only once, in 1948 when he came to Aspen for the Goethe Bicentennial celebration. Dr. Schweitzer was also an organist and connoisseur of the instrument. According to local legend, he asked if there was an organ in town he could play, and he was directed to the Aspen Community Church.

Breckenridge—Father Dyer United Methodist Church

Much has changed for Breckenridge and for its Methodist Church since the building was constructed in 1880. In 1879, Father John Dyer was assigned to the Breckenridge Circuit and he moved to Breckenridge. Since there was no church or parsonage, he purchased a lot on French Street and gave part of it to the church trustees. He built much of the church structure himself; in its original form it was a simple box-like, schoolhouse shape.

After preaching his first sermon in the new church, Father Dyer left his full-time assignment in Breckenridge. Heartbroken after the murder of his son Elias, the indomitable pastor was

Father Dyer United Methodist Church in Breckenridge

slowing down at age 67, yet could not afford to retire. It had been a difficult assignment, in a territory so large as to be almost unmanageable. He wrote, "This was a year of toil, and no pay to speak of . . . ," then an astonishing statement, ". . . did more hard work than I ever did before. . . ." Yet at the end of his career he could still say, "I never enjoyed myself better any place" than Summit County.

Father Dyer did come back to Breckenridge's Methodist Church in 1885 as interim pastor for two years. During his time there he arranged for a colorful, very effective lady evangelist to speak in the church. The widow Maggie Van Cott was the first woman licensed to preach in the Methodist Episcopal Church, according to Jane Morton's entertaining history, "Dyer, Dynamite & Dredges."

Another pastor was colorful in name but controversial in style. The Reverend Florida Passmore succeeded in pressuring the sheriff to enforce a state law which required saloons to close on Sunday. Newcomer Passmore found himself meddling in the sacred right of miners to spend their only day off hanging out in their favorite watering holes. It didn't take long for a mysterious force to retaliate by dynamiting the new belfry of the Methodist Church. Townspeople expressed their shock by collecting money to replace the bell, and according to local tradition reported by Jane Morton, ". . . those who contributed the most were the ones responsible for the damage." Culprits were never apprehended, but it is likely that local residents knew who they were. A few months later, Sunday business was back to normal in Breckenridge saloons. For a few more years Passmore continued his antagonistic posture toward other sacred cows of the community, which resulted in his being hanged in effigy, and eventually the Methodist Conference dismissed him.

The church's well-being was touch-and-go for the boom-and-bust years that followed. Through it all was the stout-hearted Ladies Aid Society, which historically played a vital role as benefactor and stabilizer of struggling churches and communities all across America. By 1965, Breckenridge was in another recovery mode, this time as a ski resort, but the Methodist church was barely alive and about to close its doors. Then, the Reverend

Mark Fiester, a Denver minister already awed by the Dyer epic, volunteered to take on the challenge of a small, deteriorating church in Breckenridge. Fiester and his wife, Roberta, were willing to dedicate their energies and resources to revitalizing this ministry—so rich in heritage, so deserving of another chance.

During the Fiesters' pastorate (1965–1972) a remarkable range of modernizing and aesthetic improvements were made, new traditions established, and the church grew again. In 1966, the name was changed to Father Dyer United Methodist Church. By 1977, the culminating event that verified the church's good health was the endeavor to move the building to a new, larger site on Briar Rose Lane. Facilities have since been enlarged considerably.

To preserve a link to its unique past, new leaded-glass windows were installed in 1979. They are memorials that make reference to various aspects of the church's long ministry. Father Dyer's familiar attributes are pictured in three windows featuring miners' tools, a Bible, the plain little church he helped to build, the itinerant pastor on skis, and the most distinctive window ever placed in a church—Father Dyer preaching in a saloon. Inside the church is a mounted cross made from a ski pole and one of Father Dyer's homemade Norwegian snowshoes.

Breckenridge—St. John's Episcopal Church

Part of the Breckenridge Historic District, St. John's Episcopal Church was built by Congregationalists in 1880 and transferred to the Episcopalians in 1891. Later the building was moved to its present location.

Breckenridge, not a common name, was altered from John C. Breckinridge of Kentucky, who served as vice-president under James Buchanan (1857–1861). The little Colorado mining camp founded in 1859 by an Alabaman was given the vice-president's

In March of 1892 the town received electricity, and two days later lights were turned on in St. John's—the first congregation in Breckenridge to be "electrified."

name. In 1860, Breckinridge ran as a pro-slavery candidate in the presidential election and was defeated by Abraham Lincoln. When the Civil War began, John Breckinridge became a Confederate general and later joined the Confederate Cabinet as Secretary of War. The town of Breckenridge's pro-Union residents apparently wished to dissociate their town from the person whose name they had honored, and they petitioned Congress to change it. A simple modification in spelling resulted. (One wonders if the early townspeople were mollified by a mere replacement of an *i* with an *e*.)

One of the most famous and dedicated circuit riders of the Colorado frontier was John Dyer, a Methodist minister known as "Father" Dyer. He built a tiny log church in 1857 in the mining town of Fairplay. It burned down in 1873 along with many other buildings. A duplicate of that little church, built around 1880, was eventually moved to South Park City Museum where it stands as a memorial to the early circuit riders, especially John L. Dyer.

The church bell that rings each Sunday in Golden's Calvary Episcopal Church was donated by Mrs. George Jarvis in 1870 when the belfry was added to the church front. (Photo by Thomas Messinger)

Golden—Calvary Episcopal Church

The town of Golden and its Calvary Episcopal Church have important historical connections. Golden City was started in Clear Creek Canyon in 1859 during the Rush to the Rockies for gold. The settlement had the resources and leadership to compete with Denver as a major supply center and for political prominence; Golden was the territorial capital from 1862–1867. Calvary Episcopal was completed in 1867, making it the oldest remaining downtown church in Golden and one of the oldest in the state.

Bishop George Randall had close ties to Golden and assisted in the effort to organized and build this church, as well as laying its cornerstone. He also established a school for boys in Golden, Jarvis Hall, which was deeded to the Territory in 1874 and eventually became Colorado School of Mines.

Some other names well known to Coloradoans are associated

with Calvary Episcopal. Adolph Coors, Sr. (Coors Brewery) donated the pews still in use today. The original vestry included such prominent citizens as W.A.H. Loveland, one of the town's founders and builder of Colorado Central Railroad. Loveland was church treasurer and reputed to have met the greater part of the church's obligations out of his own pocket.

Another distinguished vestry member was Capt. Edward L. Berthoud, Swiss-born surveyor, engineer, and a founder of Golden who also taught at the School of Mines. A small northern Colorado town is named for him as well as the scenic mountain pass he discovered which opened travel to Salt Lake City.

Lake City—Lake City Baptist

This postcard-perfect structure is a carefully crafted version of Carpenter Gothic. In 1891, more than a decade after the simpler Presbyterian and St. Rose of Lima churches, generous use of decoration on the Baptist Church reflects the more ornamented styling of its time as well as increased prosperity of the community. The church's Tiffany stained-glass windows imported from France were the first leaded glass church windows in Lake City.

Ironically, the church was built near the red-light district, but

Lake City Baptist Church. Note decorated, irregular forms, vertical lines, and steep angles characteristic of the Gothic Revival style. Details are enhanced by contrasting blue trim.

it has outlived those competitors down the street. Like so many churches in the mining centers, when mining activity slowed and the community faded, the Baptist Church also went through a period of deterioration and declining membership. Following its revival in the 1960s and 1970s it remains the only church in Lake City still in its original form, unmodified except for an addition to accommodate a kitchen and fellowship activities.

Lake City—St. Rose of Lima

The three featured churches in Lake City are similar in style with their tall single spires, angular silhouettes, and colorful wooden exteriors. The sharp steeples seem to echo Lake City's dramatic setting high among the San Juan peaks. Yet each church is quite different in overall appearance.

St. Rose of Lima was the second church built on Colorado's Western Slope of the Rockies. It was named for the first canonized saint of the Americas and finished late in 1877—just a year after George Darley's Presbyterian church. For several years spanning the turn of the century, its support came from one of

The "new" old St. Rose of Lima in Lake City

the ethnic pockets often found in mining communities—in this case, Italian miners from nearby Henson, west of Lake City on Henson Creek.

This striking church, on an elevated site overlooking the town, had a near brush with demolition in the 1980s. What began as a simple intent to replace peeling wallpaper in the sanctuary led to discovery of serious structural problems caused by a weakened foundation. This condition had caused walls to shift, threatening to collapse the walls and roof. The cost for major renovation, necessary to keep from losing the structure, was difficult for the small congregation to manage. It took a few years to accumulate funds to complete the restoration, and help came from throughout the United States. The staggering scope of the project cost over $50,000 and involved what amounted to virtually constructing a new church: new foundation; removal and replacement of the sagging roof; renovation of the spire; rewiring; insulation; new heating; painting the interior and exterior; installation of a new floor; new lighting fixtures; and reinstallation of stained-glass windows.

Lake City can be proud of its efforts to preserve and maintain these charming architectural ties to its own colorful past and to Colorado's unique nineteenth-century heritage.

Ouray—First Presbyterian Church

The Ouray church George Darley built has a story of its own. By 1883, the congregation had dwindled to the point that it was unable to make payment on the outstanding note of barely $300. The property was sold to Father Machebeuf at a sheriff's sale for $325 and renamed St. Patrick's. In 1954, when St. Patrick's parish was ready for a new church, the old structure was sawed in half and moved 80 miles over the mountains to Nucla where it is in use as Our Lady of Sorrows.

In 1887, the Ouray Presbyterians reorganized; by 1890, they built a new church on a different lot, from a design illustrated in

First Presbyterian Church in Ouray

a plan book provided by the Presbyterian Board of Church Erection. George Darley came from Fort Morgan to dedicate the new church and greet old friends; he was to become its pastor eight years later. As for the structure itself, there are no records of construction details. Later additions were made which modified the front entrance, and the building was raised off its foundation in order to build a basement. The steeple featured in the original plan was never built; the present bell tower dates from the 1950s.

A number of outstanding pastors and community leaders have been involved in the survival of this gem tucked into the magnificent San Juan Mountains. Roger Henn, Ouray historian, has written a thorough account of the uphill and downhill life of Ouray and its Presbyterians; *In Journeyings Often* (1993) was the source of much of the historical information contained in this description.

Leadville—Catholic Community

A prosaic name like Leadville belies the high-spirited life that went on there during its days as a mining boomtown. In its prime during the late 1870s and 1880s, Leadville was Colorado's second city after Denver. Leadville's reputation exploited its bawdy side, but there was also culture and a taste for finer things. Hard-working, clean-living residents had their corner among bigger-than-life personalities like Horace and Baby Doe Tabor, J. J. Brown and the Unsinkable Molly. In 1878, there were four churches among its 120 saloons, 19 beer halls and 118 gambling houses.

St. Joseph's Church in Leadville

That could be considered a lot of churches or not enough, depending on one's aspirations for the town.

The story of Leadville's churches can be told in terms of its diverse ethnic population. St. Joseph's is a product of Slovenian immigration that began for Leadville in 1883. Other Slavic people from Croatia, Dalmatia, and Slovakia also came to work, as merchants as well as miners. They were bonded by their common language and heritage as part of what was then the Austrian Empire. And they had exotic *k*- and *z*-filled Slavic names. In 1896, Bishop Nicholas Matz sent a Slovenian-speaking priest, Father John Perse, to the Church of the Annunciation to help the "Austrians."

"The Old Church", originally First Presbyterian—one of Leadville's distinctive towers.

In 1880, the cornerstone of St. George's Episcopal Church in Leadville was laid.
When finished, the building was a small version of St. George's in New York
City. Hand-hewn timbers form its Gothic arches, and the bell, a gift from famous "Silver King" H. A. W. Tabor, still announces every Sunday service. Early
in its history, this parish started a school when there was not enough financial
support to keep the public schools open. (Photo by Thomas Messinger)

Since Annunciation was primarily an Irish congregation, Father
Perse organized a separate parish, St. Joseph's, for the Slovenian
Austrians and began construction for a church in 1899.

The attention given to the cornerstone-laying on December 17
was typical of those ceremonies for community-sponsored buildings of the time, such as courthouses and churches. On that mid-
December afternoon, at 10,000 feet elevation with the ground
covered with snow, it must have been a chilly walk for those who
took part in the grand procession through town from Annunciation, down Harrison Avenue to the building site. The Leadville
Miners Band managed to play even though their fingers were
stiff and their instruments were filling with ice. Bishop Cyril
Zupan of Pueblo addressed the group in their native language. A

few weeks later in February, 1900, the first Mass in St. Joseph's was celebrated, presumably by its pastor Father Perse.

One night in March, 1923, the church caught fire. In the strong arctic wind and subzero temperature, fighting the blaze was hopeless, and the building burned to the ground. The very next day the stunned congregation met and made plans to build a new church. With heroic effort, they raised $30,000 by July 1, and the new cornerstone was laid on August 13. This ceremony was once again cause for great celebration.

The church we see today was ready for its first Mass on Christmas Eve, 1923. The church wasn't finished, however, and worshipers had to stand. Nor was the bell installed yet, so two men struck it with a hammer; the unconventional sound must have been attention-getting but most welcome under the circumstances. Less than a year after its devastating setback, this plucky parish was back on track again with a monumental, new, brick church.

One of those who worked most diligently soliciting funds to rebuild the church was Anton Koroshetz, St. Joseph's organist and choir director for 26 years from about 1905. A serious-looking man with a big black wing mustache, Koroshetz was also Austrian-born. He was a highly-trained professional and totally dedicated to his music ministry in Leadville. He also found time to organize a Slovenian glee club, a handsome group of 20 high-collared young men which included the town constable.

Three of the Slovenian-speaking clergy from the early days also deserve special mention. Much-loved Father Perse was the right person for the job at the right time. He was a highly capable organizer and administrator and had a reputation for fastidious maintenance of the church. He was well educated and multi-lingual, a young man with considerable vision whose early life had been one of continual struggle. As a very young lad he made the journey to America in the care of a drunkard who didn't bother to feed him.

Father Judnic was also a young man when assigned to St. Joseph's in 1915. He was highly regarded as an intellectual and as a modest and very saintly man. A story is told that Father Judnic refused money raised by some parishioners because it came from the surreptitious sale of homemade wine at a church fundraiser. Needing money badly, he later relented.

As for Father George M. Trunck, few individuals require quite so many lines to lay out a brief biographical sketch as this intrepid Renaissance man. He was a priest in his native Carinthia for 25 years before moving to America in 1920 at age 50. He had already traveled to the United States four times as a tourist, and on one such trip in 1909 he passed through Leadville. During World War I he was imprisoned by the Austrian government on suspicion of being a spy because of his visits to America. Later he was part of the peace delegation to Versailles. In addition to an active role in politics and diplomacy, he was a journalist, editor, author, accomplished linguist, and artist. He decorated the interior walls and ceiling of St. Joseph's with religious murals, doing the last in his 77th year. Father Trunck began his ministry in Leadville in 1924 and left in 1946. In the church history book there is a photograph of 100-year-old Father Trunck, in his clerical collar, smiling and holding a lighted cigar. Not an ordinary man. He died in 1972 at age 102.

Silverton—St. Patrick's Catholic Church

When Bishop Joseph Machebeuf came to Silverton in 1883 to organize the building of St. Patrick's Catholic Church, a train ride from Denver would take nearly 30 hours—when it ran on time. That same year the peripatetic cleric returned for the

Silverton Baptist Church, 1898. The ubiquitous Otto Mears went to his final resting place from his funeral in this church—at that time Episcopalian. Mears, the enterprising and fearless builder of railroads and mountain toll roads, figures in local histories of early Colorado in many ways, which were not always exemplary; he was suspected of providing a horse and money for the dastardly Alferd Packer's escape from the Saguache jail.

church's dedication and again a few months later! The winter of the bishop's visits was exceptionally severe. Several people were killed by avalanches, and the railroad was blocked for 73 days by deep snow. Food and supplies ran low under such circumstances, but none of this was uncommon during Silverton's winters.

That first, frame church on Quality Hill was moved twice after it was built, and purchased later by the African Methodist congregation. The present, Norman-style brick building was erected in 1905. A largely Catholic, multi-ethnic local population of His-

St. Patrick's in Silverton has undergone a number of improvements and renovation projects. The church interior has been particularly enriched by several pieces of the wood artistry of Carl Schubert of Grand Junction.

panics, Welsh, Italians, Austrians, and Slavs donated the construction knowing their lives would be intertwined with what the church gave back to them. For in this region of stunning natural beauty and capricious, often life-threatening weather, drama was part of daily life, and men of the cloth experienced more than their share while tending their flocks in the perilous world of mining.

Father Cornelius O'Rourke was one of those assigned to St. Patrick's. No doubt a hardy fellow, he had been a miner. He also built the first Catholic church at Telluride and was planning the new, brick St. Patrick's. This popular young priest was thrown from his horse into the Las Animas River and drowned. His long-time friend John McComb also drowned while trying to save him, and the community mourned this double loss. Another priest, Father Kleinbrecht was a German immigrant who served St. Patrick's from 1911–1914. He was obliged to leave Colorado in 1914 to serve with the German military forces, as he hadn't been in America long enough to become a U.S. citizen and was still a reserve in the Kaiser's army. According to the *Silverton Standard,* he was considered "one of the best-liked priests in Colorado." There is no mention of his fate in the Great War.

In 1959, at a time when mining activity was minimal in Silverton, a group from the Men's Club of St. Patrick's placed a monumental statue of Christ on Anvil Mountain as a shrine to miners and to the wavering industry they represented. Donations and support came from diverse sources, and it was indeed an ambitious project, with emotional overtones. The 12-foot sculpture was carved in Italy of Carrara marble and placed in a man-made alcove looking down over Silverton. Its candlelight dedication procession on an August evening must have been inspiring to all who participated. Soon after, the mining industry around Silverton revived.

Cripple Creek and Victor Mining District

There were 34 active churches established in the first ten years after the discovery of gold in the Cripple Creek and Victor Mining District. One that remains is St. Peter's Catholic Church, easily spotted on the highest hill in Cripple Creek. Begun in the boom days of one of the world's greatest gold mining camps, the parish soon outgrew its original tiny frame building. In 1892, Father T. Volpe was sent by Bishop Nicholas Matz of Denver to minister to the faithful in the fabulous and then-thriving mining district. Volpe was old and quite sickly but he lasted for five years in the rugged, hilly town at 9,000 feet on the western side of

St. Peter's

St. Victor's Church in Victor

Pikes Peak. He celebrated Easter High Mass in the new St. Peter's in 1898 and then his health gave out. The parish barely survived the impacts of World War I, the falling price of gold, and a terrible influenza epidemic. Cripple Creek became an authentic ghost town.

A similar fate befell St. Victor's Catholic Church in Victor, another town in the District. It had 350 Catholic families in 1903 when it was built to replace a wooden structure. But the vagaries of the boom towns took their toll. In 1928, the parishes of St. Peter's and St. Victor's were joined as one community. Following World War II, they came under the care of Colorado Springs parishes.

Today the Catholic community worships at St. Victor's in the winter and St. Peter's in the summer as missions of Our Lady of the Woods in Woodland Park.

Bishop John Franklin Spaulding established the Episcopal cathedral form of government for Episcopal parishes in the ten-year-old State of Colorado in 1886. He was responsible for the beginnings of

St. Andrew's Episcopal Church in Cripple Creek

First Baptist Church in Cripple Creek

St. Andrew's, a small mission church in Cripple Creek. A one-time cowboy then Episcopalian priest, Father Charles Grimes was assigned to the fledgling congregation in 1893. In November of the same year, the first service was held in the new brick St. Andrew's. Soon there were over 100 parishioners.

Then came disaster. In April of 1896 most of Cripple Creek burned down in a devastating fire and St. Andrew's was a casualty. The bell was the only thing left. It was carefully stored away, to be rediscovered in 1957. Meanwhile St. Andrew's and Cripple Creek rose from the ashes, and both prospered for a time. Later, with the fall of gold prices and World War I the district's economy faltered. Services were turned over to visiting missionaries. In 1958, St. Andrew's became a parish again with a resident priest.

Cripple Creek is now making a comeback as a gambling center, but behind the refurbished facades are the real remnants of yesteryear—including the symbols of its pioneer churchgoers.

Salida's First Christian Church (Disciples of Christ)

Salida—First Christian Church
(Disciples of Christ)

One of the most democratic of ecclesiastical organizations, the Christian Church (Disciples of Christ) is well represented throughout Colorado. Followers were often known as Stoneites or Campbellites, in reference to originators of the denomination, who believed local congregations should govern themselves.

Disciple followers organized in Salida in 1882 when the town was just two years old. A series of brief pastorates followed during the early years, but a small, active and devoted membership kept the church alive and growing. The first pastor had forged credentials, and after a series of indiscretions left town in disgrace. Fortunately, his successors have consisted of a number of multi-talented, benevolent, and infinitely more respectable members of the clergy.

A simple white frame church was built in 1888 which provided a baptistry underneath the floor. Prior to having their own church, communicants used the Arkansas River for baptisms. Now, in summer everyday including Sunday, the turbulent Arkansas at Salida is one of the country's most challenging and popular white-water rafting rivers.

In 1906, a revival-meeting appearance by the famous evangelist Reverend William A. "Billy" Sunday increased Salida's number of saved souls by 612, and the Christian Church absorbed over 100 of these. Soon after, plans were made for a larger house of worship. The white church was moved, and a new, brick building took its place. The brick church burned in 1934 in a fire that did minor damage to the Methodist Church nearby.

Despite the difficulties of the Depression, the Christian Church was rebuilt with support and interim assistance from other Salida churches and organizations, and from the City of Salida. Modifications to the burned-out, red-brick, steep-gabled structure gave the new version quite a different style from its predecessor. With slightly different contours, a flat roofline, and light-colored exterior, the rebuilt church has acquired a distinctive, rather Moorish look. Such uniqueness in outer form seems complementary to the independence and flexibility which characterized the denomination's beginnings.

The cornerstone for the First Baptist Church near
downtown Salida was laid in 1885. The building was
remodeled and enlarged in 1921 to its present
configuration.

Jefferson Community Church

The little jewel that is now Jefferson Community Church was originally built as the town's schoolhouse in 1902. Religious activities were held in the school even at that time. The school bell, which students' contributions helped to purchase, also called to Sunday worshipers as it still does. When the first Sunday school was organized, Jesse Carruthers, who built the schoolhouse, served as its first superintendent.

Father Dyer may have been the first preacher to visit Jefferson long before the schoolhouse was built. Several years later, a local resident, Howard Wright, recalled that when he was a teenager,

Jefferson Community Church (Photo by Jean Messinger)

Father Dyer stayed in the Wright home. It was young Howard's job to take Father Dyer around in his buggy, and he remembered the famous preacher as a large man on crutches.

Services and Sunday school were sporadic during the following years. Some visiting preachers came 80 miles from Denver to bring "Sunday" to this very small group of worshipers. In 1944, the school district was consolidated and local children were bused to Fairplay. By 1949, a successful effort was made to organize the congregation, and the church doors have been open ever since.

Delta's United Presbyterian Church

Delta—United Presbyterian Church

Delta Presbyterians were organized as a mission in 1884 by Sheldon Jackson. A small group of about a dozen worshipers were served by the Reverend T. S. Day, who rode his horse from Grand Junction once a month. On each 40-mile journey Day had to cross the Gunnison River several times, and it is recorded that "he arrived wet several times but never drowned."

The mission church was under George Darley while he was at Lake City, and from 1906 to 1911 Darley served as pastor. Another of the church's inspiring ministers was H. J. Frothinham. Well-educated and sophisticated, the Reverend Frothinham was a community leader and a man of many talents. It was he who promoted and organized the building of the present structure in 1901. His brother in Chicago donated 18 handmade oak pews, which are still in use. In a domain where personnel tenures are often brief, Shirley Hodgin played the church's Pennsylvania-made organ for 46 years from 1936 until 1980.

The brick exterior of Delta's United Presbyterian was stuccoed in 1963. Its stark white surface enhances the building's simple, dramatic lines. Dominated by the solid tower and steeply-pitched roof, it is a handsome, almost contemporary-looking church.

Eckert Presbyterian Church. Through the years of World War I and the influenza epidemic of 1919, men, women and children of Eckert gathered native lava rock, the residue of ancient volcanic eruptions. In 1921, they were formally able to build their church from this unusual material.

Olathe Baptist Church

Olathe Baptist Church

The structure that is Olathe's Baptist Church was originally a small chapel on the hill outside of town, where a handful of believers worshiped and organized in 1885. The building was moved into town in 1896 and has since been enlarged and remodeled as the church's needs have grown. The organ was given by a couple in celebration of their 60th wedding anniversary.

A touching story from this church reveals the characteristic dedication and sincerity of many of the early clergy, as well as their impoverished situation. An itinerant minister called Father Clark helped to organize the five charter members of the chapel on the hill. He was known to walk barefoot from town to town, carrying his shoes in order to save them for church.

The church's original name was Colorow Baptist Church, as the town was also called Colorow—a Shawnee word meaning "fine, beautiful." Colorow was also a well-known Ute chief. Changing names was a common pattern in Colorado's early settlements, and reasons varied. By 1896, the renegade chief's reputation included suspicion that he had murdered Nathan Meeker during the White River Indian Agency (Meeker) Massacre in 1879. This disturbed local residents enough to change the town's name to Olathe, after a town in Kansas. Not until 1954 did the Colorow Baptist Church follow suit.

A unique cross with its well-kept secret tops Meeker's St. James Episcopal Church. In yet another demonstration of institutional flexibility, in the early days this church was closed for the month of June to allow fishermen "to play hooky from church with clear conscience."

Meeker—St. James Episcopal Church

A visit to Meeker requires a short diversion north of Rifle from I-70. Meeker is a pleasant and peaceful town on the White River, a place that belies its historical association with Nathan Meeker and the massacre at the White River Indian Agency in 1879.

St. James has importance of its own. In the 1880s, Meeker's population included many English people who wanted their own church. After meeting regularly in the old hospital building, a group managed to collect $600, enough money to start an Episcopalian church in 1888. The newly-arrived Reverend Arthur Williams pitched right in, helping to dig the foundation and to lay the stones quarried from nearby Flag Creek. The church was finished the following year and rarely seems to have been without a building project ever since.

This congregation has been fortunate to have had some ministers who were especially ambitious for the church and provided aggressive and inspiring leadership. Nor were they above rolling up their sleeves alongside construction crews. Arthur Williams was such a man. Even after he became bishop of Nebraska, he maintained an interest in the affairs of St. James and an affection for his beginnings there. In 1908, Bishop Williams was in Washington at the time of the cornerstone-laying ceremony for the Episcopal cathedral. When he was introduced to the speaker, President Theodore Roosevelt, the president was surprised to greet the man whose name he had encountered while bear hunting near Meeker. In fact, during that visit he attended services at St. James. Throwing his arm around Bishop Williams' shoulder, he said, ". . . I know all about you; the people up there haven't quit talking about that man Williams who did things out there in the early days. I'm mighty glad to meet you, Sir!"

Thereupon the president and the bishop lapsed into a nostalgic conversation about adventure in the Wild West. It isn't recorded which one was more impressed by that surprise meeting between the sportsman president and the prelate from the West.

Another beloved pastor was Father W. O. Richards, who served Meeker and surrounding parishes and missions for 37 years. A charming story from those years surfaced not long ago. It seems that when Richards arrived in Meeker in 1931 to take over St. James' ministry, the cross had fallen off the top of the bell tower. Mrs. Richards, who claimed credit for keeping the secret of its repair, tells it best:

> . . . [T]here was a farmer here, a Roman Catholic, who was a sheet metal worker. He came to my husband and said he knew where he could get some copper to cover the Cross and to replace the rotted wood in the Church Tower so that the Bell could be hung there without falling through the roof. It was at the time of the Prohibition years and this person knew where there was a liquor "still," and he could get the copper there, but this was to be kept a deep secret, which was kept. He did the work free of

charge . . . But now, since all concerned except Fr. Richards have passed to their reward, the secret can be told.

Both Richardses have passed away (in their 90s), and revelation of the cross's origin is probably met with less shock than approval for such resourceful recycling.

Rico Community Church

Rico is a mountain community of about 100 people, 24 miles south of Telluride on scenic Highway 145. The Community Church was originally called People's Church of Rico, and indeed it was just that. At the time it was built in 1890, Rico was a mining boomtown of 4000 folks who had no organized church. But leave it to the ladies—the Ladies Church Building Organization literally canvassed door-to-door soliciting money and promises of time and labor to build a church for Rico. Even land was donated. In a year the building was finished at a cost of $4000 and dedicated in February, 1891. For many years it was the only church in town.

Rico community Church

Near Rico, the Johnson Memorial United Methodist Church in Dolores just may be the only historic church in Colorado that owes its beginnings to a race horse. Mary Johnson's husband had a thoroughbred that brought in a good deal of money from races he won in the East. In 1908 Mrs. Johnson donated $5000 from his winnings so that construction on a Methodist church could begin. And so she is memorialized in its name.

The people of Rico are still very proud of their church, and their commitment to its maintenance shows. It has been extensively renovated but not modified from its original form. Several features are distinctive and the originals are still in place, such as the bell (1892), a pump organ (still operating), clear glass windows, roll-up partitions, and an elaborately carved altar.

Church members also speak with affection of the missionary pastor who served them for 12 years during the 1970s and 80s. He was the Reverend Carl Dickson, who came to Rico for Sunday afternoon services from the Presbyterian Church in Towaoc. Towaoc is on the Ute Mountain Indian Reservation in the Four Corners area, south of Cortez. Dickson was a Nez Perce Indian ministering to an almost entirely Anglo congregation. He is remembered as "a fine preacher" and "an outstanding person."

Using local sandstone quarried from Horse Gulch, the congregation of St. Mark's in Durango did their best to insure that their church would never again be consumed by fire.

Durango—St. Mark's Episcopal Church

So much was demanded of frontier churchmen in order to survive and to lead that the frontier was not a place for weaklings or even mediocrity. Perhaps that is why the annals give us such larger-than-life personalities as George Darley and C. Montgomery Hogue. "Parson" Hogue was more than the folk hero who strode into saloons wearing his cassock and six-shooters. A reformed gambler, bold, individualistic, confident, and using his huge frame to advantage, he was a difficult force to ignore or resist. One of the most colorful characters of southwest Colorado, Parson Hogue came from "accounts disagree" and went on to "no one's quite sure." In the interim he ministered in the Wet Mountain Valley, and by the late 1870s showed up in the San Juans. He preached and established missions around Telluride, in Ouray, Mancos, and Rico, and in 1880 established St. Mark's

Mission in Durango. His worship services in the dining room of the Delmonico Hotel on the day after Christmas 1880 are described as "the first of their kind ever held in Durango."

The following year the Parson worked alongside his followers to build a church. That church burned when much of Durango went up in flames in the fire of 1889. Parson Hogue was long gone by then, but the congregation resolved immediately to rebuild. This scenario was repeated many times on the frontier where lightning was a frequent devastator, and relentless winds and short water supply made fire fighting a one-sided, losing battle. People watched their towns burn but it seldom deterred their vision for a future in that same location.

By early 1892 the present structure was ready on new lots purchased before the fire. St. Mark's has recently undergone extensive restoration, and it was surprising to learn the church is over 100 years old.

Marble—Marble Community Church

Marble is tucked into a particularly scenic spot in Colorado's mountains—peaks with straightforward names like Sheep, Hat, and Chair. This historic town is on the Crystal River, with views of spectacular Mt. Sopris along the way up from Carbondale. The area's heritage is as rich as its mineral resources and natural beauty. But its main claim to fame is its enormous quarry of pure white marble. In its heyday this quarry produced a 65-ton block that was shipped to Vermont, carved down to 56 tons, and in-

The steeple and bell were added in 1912, after the building was moved from Aspen. As Marble's Community Church, it has since been renovated and modernized and placed on the National Register of Historic Places.

stalled at the Tomb of the Unknown in Arlington Cemetery. In fact, marble from Marble was used in courthouses, post offices, and city halls around the country. In 1915 scores of railroad flat-car-loads of the beautiful crystalline stone were delivered to Washington, D.C. for use in the Lincoln Memorial.

Marble itself has experienced that rollercoaster economy common to Colorado's mining communities, and its people have exhibited the resilience required for survival in such demanding circumstances. Settlement of the Crystal River Valley began during the 1880s, largely by prospectors moving down Schofield Pass from Crested Butte. By 1908, Marble was a thriving settlement of 1000 residents, largely Italian and East European immigrants. Organized religion was represented by a large and active Sunday school and visits by itinerant preachers, but not by a church building.

Meanwhile, mining activity in Aspen had declined, and St. John's Episcopal Chapel, built there in 1888, was no longer needed. The building was dismantled and brought on a flatbed car up the riverside rail line to Marble, where the arrival of stacks of building components were cause for excitement among townspeople.

Two side rooms were added at this time. Renamed St. Paul's, the church became the community religious, social, and cultural center. It even contained a reading room with small library, and a boys' club behind the church. At 7950 feet, winters are long and white; at times the church was so fully booked that some religious activities had to be held at other venues.

Episcopalians, Congregationalists, and Catholics all held separate services here. The Catholics tried to build their own church in 1912, but heavy snow collapsed the wood superstructure, and the building was never completed. Its abandoned foundation of white marble blocks stand in the forest like Greek temple ruins. In the 1930s, Father McSweeney used to come by train from Aspen every Sunday afternoon. But he believed people should not have to disrupt Sunday by having to go to church on their only day off from work, so he said Mass on Monday mornings before the day shift at the mill.

Both World Wars closed the quarries and mill. For a few years,

Theresa Herman was the single resident of Marble ("after the Orloskys moved across the lake").

During the 1950s and 1960s the community and surrounding area revived, with new activity at the quarries plus developing interest in skiing and summer tourism. A new congregation formed, calling itself Marble Community Church. In 1985, the deed to St. Paul's was presented by the Episcopal Diocese to the Community congregation.

St. Patrick's Catholic Church in Minturn dates from 1913

The Bible Church in Yampa (Photo by Thomas Messinger)

Palmer Lake's Little Log Church

Palmer Lake—Little Log Church

A good example of a 1920s vernacular building, the Little Log Church was originally Friends' Community Church. A Quaker missionary, Miss Evalina Macy served the congregation from 1930 to 1959, but she was not officially made a minister until 1939.

Miss Macy encouraged the first Palmer Lake Yule Log hunt in 1933. To this day, families of the area join in the Christmas-time hunt for the evergreen log that is hidden ahead of time. When found, the log is brought to the Town Hall where half is burned in the big fireplace. The other half is saved and used to start the next year's fire.

The first yule log ceremony in the United States was held in Lake Placid, New York, and a splinter from it was sent to Palmer Lake for its first ceremony. Since then Palmer Lake has sent splinters around the country to towns where new ceremonies have been initiated.

Colorado Springs—Mothers Chapel

By congressional act on February 4, 1914, Mothers Day was made a national holiday to be celebrated on the second Sunday of each May. Building on that proclamation and embracing all faiths, the American Mothers Committee was established in 1935. Its first honorary chairperson was Mrs. Sara Delano Roosevelt, mother of President Franklin D. Roosevelt. State committees were formed beginning in 1943 in order to recognize prospective candidates for Mother of the Year.

In 1973, the American Mothers Committee petitioned the City

The tiny "Mothers Chapel" is dwarfed by its spectacular Pikes Peak backdrop.

of Colorado Springs for land on which to build a small chapel where people could come "from far and near to visit, meditate and sing." A permit was granted for a site on the city's White House Ranch, a living history park. Today, the tiny, well-cared-for white chapel is often used for weddings. Its spectacular backdrop is the Garden of the Gods Park and Pikes Peak.

Cascade—The Chapel of the Holy Rosary

The Chapel of the Holy Rosary in Cascade was built by the Frank Cusak family. Its first mass was celebrated by Archbishop Vehr of Denver in 1931. High up in Ute Pass west of Colorado Springs, the old stage and railroad route into the mountains, this little Romanesque Catholic church was constructed of native red rock. Colorado Springs architect Charles E. Thomas designed the chapel. Inside is a carved rosewood crucifix from the famous Lang Family Studio in Oberammergau. The Langs are also known for their longtime participation in the Passion Play of that city.

Holy Rosary Chapel in Cascade

Down a winding stairway to a level beneath the chapel is a stone grotto, faithfully modeled after the Shrine of Our Lady of Lourdes in France, where apparitions of the Virgin Mary appeared to 14-year-old Bernadette Soubirous in 1858. Soft votive lights create the atmosphere of a place of devotion.

Frank Cusack donated the chapel to the Catholic diocese. It is now a mission of the Parish of Sacred Heart in Colorado Springs and serves several mountain communities in the area.

Green Mountain Falls—Church in the Wildwood

The old summer resort town of Green Mountain Falls lies against the mountains in Ute Pass, a gateway through the Front Range of the Rockies. Even before a church was built, it was common for Sunday afternoon services for summer visitors to be held in the town park. On one such occasion some 2000 people gathered there to hear a sermon by Reverend T. DeWitt Talmadge of Brooklyn, no less.

The Congregational Church of Christ was built in 1889. Because the year-round population was only 40, the church was not

Green Mountain Falls' Church in the Wildwood

equipped for winter in the mountains. It wasn't until the winter of 1949–1950 that proper heating was installed.

Much has been added to the original brown-shingled sanctuary over the years, including a new name, but the heart of the church remains visible. Visitors and residents alike cherish this little town and its historic place of worship.

Our Lady of Perpetual Help in Manitou Springs

Manitou Springs—Our Lady of Perpetual Help

In 1882 the indomitable French missionary, Bishop Joseph Machebeuf established a Catholic parish in Manitou (now Manitou Springs). A church was completed and dedicated in 1889. In 1893 Father Jean Baptiste Francolon, a French priest seeking a health cure from local mineral springs, took over the parish. The son of a wealthy family, Francolon proceeded to build a castle near his church. The castle, which he called Miramont, was modeled after European sites Francolon had visited in his youth.

Quintessentially eclectic, the castle represents no fewer than nine architectural styles, and very few rooms have the customary four walls. Francolon and his mother took up residence in the castle and then quite suddenly left in 1900. Undoubtedly, Our Lady of Perpetual help is the only parish in Colorado—perhaps in the country—whose pastor built and resided in an honest-to-goodness castle.

In 1903, the little church burned down, but in the same year

the present structure, built by Angus and Archibald Gillis, replaced it. The dollhouse-like Our Lady of Perpetual Help is now
a mission of Sacred Heart Parish in Colorado Springs, and Miramont Castle belongs to the Manitou Springs Historical Society.
Father Ted Haas, a grandson of Angus Gillis, is Rector Emeritus
of St. Mary's Cathedral in Colorado Springs.

Miramont, Manitou Springs' own castle

Manitou Springs—St. Andrew's Episcopal Church

The Episcopal congregation of Manitou, a town nestled at the foot of Pikes Peak, began with services held in a tent in 1874. The land was donated by Dr. William Bell, one of Manitou's planners. In 1880, a small wooden church was built near Fountain Creek. After a serious flood, the damaged church was moved to the "safer" side of the creek, and it served the Episcopalian community for some 23 years.

A local business had donated a stone wall on church property even before the new building was erected in 1904. The ever-

St. Andrew's Episcopal Church in Manitou Springs

green-surrounded, English Gothic, sandstone structure still has its memorial stained-glass windows from London, a Vermont marble altar, and a carved bishop's throne.

Original St. Andrew's building

Community Congregational Church, the oldest church building in Manitou Springs, dates from 1880. Originally called First Congregational, the church was constructed of native stone from the quarry of George Snyder, who served as contractor along with Angus Gillis, local stonemason and builder. The influence of early English settlers and promoters can be seen in the traditional English Gothic windows, main entrance, and bell tower. In 1922 the church became the Community Congregational and so it remains today. An inscription over the entrance reads, "Thy Righteousness is Like the Great Mountains."

Chapel on the Rock near Estes Park

Estes Park—St. Malo

Twelve miles south of Estes Park stands a large and sturdy, stone chapel with majestic Mount Meeker as its backdrop. Alpine meadows and conifer forests complete the setting. It is aptly named the "Chapel on the Rock" where services are held for the spacious St. Malo Retreat Center. How the chapel came to be built is a unique story. In August of 1916, Father Joseph Bosetti, a young assistant pastor from the Denver cathedral, was camping in the area as he loved to do. After nightfall, he was astonished by the sight of a meteor that flashed across the night sky and seemed close enough to have landed somewhere nearby. Though he searched and never found the meteorite, by dawn he came upon an immense rock formation so grand he vowed that some-day a chapel would be built there, along with a campsite. In 1935, under the direction of the Denver archdiocese, Bosetti's dream became a reality.

Later in his life and by then a monsignor, Bosetti said, "The religious atmosphere of the camp cannot fail to make an everlasting impression."

Indeed, over the years, the mountain getaway has impressed thousands of retreatants, visitors, and photographers, and in 1993 Pope John Paul II, who stayed there briefly during the World Youth Congress.

Lyons—First Congregational Church

Permanent settlers came to the St. Vrain Valley after 1860, seeking good land for farming and ranching and discovering lumber and stone resources as well. E. S. Lyon arrived around 1880, became postmaster, and platted a town site on his own 160 acres. While in Lyons, he built a one-room stone schoolhouse which was also used by church groups. It is still used in expanded form by the Lyons school district.

A group of Lyons residents meeting in that schoolhouse orga-

Known as the Old Stone Church, the Congregational Church in Lyons was built in 1894. Reference to Henry Hobson Richardson is unmistakable; the 1890s were the years of his strongest influence. Note the well-crafted stone work.

nized themselves into a Congregational church in 1889, with E. S. Lyon as one of the trustees. Apparently they chose to affiliate with the Congregationalists because of the support and leadership they were receiving at the time from Longmont's Congregational pastor, the Reverend H. E. Thayer. He continued to advise and aid the little group throughout its developmental period even though the Lyons church retained its own minister. With the limited resources of probably less than two dozen members, however, it was difficult to raise money for a minister's salary. In fact the first pastor was promised an annual salary of $1000, unusually generous and ambitious for the times, and he resigned soon after because that money was simply not forthcoming.

Clergy turnovers were frequent and continuity difficult to maintain—conditions that plagued the Lyons congregation for many years as it has many other small churches throughout the state. Consequently, it is remarkable that in 1894 Lyons parishioners managed to erect this handsome, substantial, and permanent structure so soon after they had organized. Excluding donations, the church cost over $3000 for purchases of stone, labor, and lumber. Except for a small outstanding loan, with the Reverend Thayer's help the building was dedicated free of debt.

The distinctive pink Lyons sandstone has supplied construction projects around the United States. These include buildings on the campus of the University of Colorado. Lyons' own 15 historic sandstone structures have been entered on the National Register and designated a Historic District by the Colorado Historical Society and U.S. Department of the Interior.

Lyons—United Methodist Church

Christian hymns refer to the importance of foundations; Lyons United Methodist Church has one not matched by many others. The building itself is perched atop a natural foundation of high-grade lime marble called Mexican Onyx. This solid marble outcropping rises five feet above the level of the street and is estimated to be 60 feet thick. In 1951, excavation in front of and under the church was done to build a fellowship space, Wesleyan Hall. The builder encountered a boulder so large and unyielding that it was left in place and covered with concrete.

Several other outcroppings of this same rock, which have been

United Methodist Church of Lyons (Photo by Jean Messinger)

assessed as commercially valuable, are visible around town. The rock is very hard material with beautiful banding and it takes a high polish, but commercial quarrying is not viable under present circumstances.

The Methodist Church was built in 1908 by William Rebendall at a cost of $4000. Dedication was presided over by Governor Buchtel, who was also a Methodist minister and chancellor of the University of Denver. Invitations for the ceremonies announced that on the evening preceding the dedication, ". . . [T]he Governor will deliver his famous lecture, 'the pleasantness of American life.' (sic)". Such a promise was sure to either entice or discourage attendance.

The present church serves in many ways as a community church. Several of the small towns around Lyons join together in activities with the Methodist congregation, and other denominations make use of its facilities for their Sunday services.

Peaceful Valley Memorial Chapel

Peaceful Valley Memorial Chapel

The Peaceful Valley Memorial Chapel built in 1977 is not, strictly speaking, an historic church although it may be some day. However, its style is traditional, its uniqueness is appealing, and readers won't be disappointed that it is included in this collection. Located off Highway 72 west of Lyons, the chapel can be seen from the road at certain vantage points. It is reached by walking a signposted ascending path from the road that runs by Peaceful Valley Lodge and Guest Ranch. The solitude and beauty of that short journey up the mountainside makes visiting the site a memorable and spiritual experience.

The chapel was built as a memorial to Paul F. Boehm by his son and daughter-in-law, Karl and Mabel. Paul Boehm brought his family to America from Austria just prior to World War II in a dramatic escape not unlike that of the Von Trapp family. He had a successful career in New York as an attorney and engineer, and although he never lived in Colorado, he visited frequently.

Karl Boehm settled in Colorado after World War II training at Camp Hale with the famous Tenth Mountain Division. He and Mabel bought the Peaceful Valley property, which included a small inn that had been a stagecoach stop. The day after the family moved in, the building burned down. The present complex is the result of many years of expansion and improvement from that inauspicious beginning.

Paul died in 1964 at age 70, and Karl and Mabel had this nondenominational chapel designed from sketches Karl made. He was intent on replicating the traditional, onion-domed, alpine style of his father's homeland in the mountain setting the family had adopted and loved in Colorado.

Westcliffe—Evangelical Lutheran Church

Eighty-six families, originally immigrants to Chicago from Germany, settled in the Wet Mountain Valley of Colorado in 1870. One of the settlers, known as "Grossmutter O'Graske," wrote to Lutheran authorities requesting a missionary for the colonists.

In 1872, Pastor Hilgendorf arrived in *Blumenau*, now Westcliffe, where he organized the first permanent Lutheran congregation in Colorado. Their church was constructed of aspen poles and had no windows or floor.

The present church was completed in 1917. Pastor John Reininga was both architect and builder. The story is told that when

Evangelical Lutheran Church in Westcliffe

he was working on the steeple, he hung his coat on the spire and jokingly told a local spectator it was a German flag. This was not a time for the issue of German nationalism to be raised, even in jest. According to local lore, a Denver newspaper took the matter quite seriously in an article that appeared soon afterwards.

Trinidad—Holy Trinity Church

In the year before Columbus first sailed for the New World, St. Ignatius of Loyola was born in the Basque country of Spain. He founded the Society of Jesus, which was to become one of the foremost missionary orders of the Catholic Church. In the nineteenth century its members, known as Jesuits, played a major role in tending to the spiritual needs of those who had settled in parts of Oklahoma, New Mexico, Arizona and Colorado.

A tiny adobe church was built around 1865 by pioneer Don Felipe Baca and his friends in the frontier town of Trinidad, named for Baca's daughter, whose name means Trinity. After ten

Holy Trinity Church in Trinidad

years there was a clear need for more priests and a larger church. Bishop Machebeuf of Denver enlisted the help of Jesuits who had been exiled by the Italian government. Thus it was that Holy Trinity Church in Trinidad was designed by Father Charles Pinto, S. J., the congregation's first Jesuit pastor and a native of Italy.

Finished and blessed in 1885, Holy Trinity served area Catholics, who represented over 20 different nationalities, most of whom did not speak English. They were, however, much at home in the traditional cruciform design of their church, so reminiscent of their European roots. Between 1875 and 1919, Holy Trinity Parish ministered to 60 missions throughout the countryside, usually the sites of mining camps. There are still at least six Jesuit parishes in Colorado's southern diocese of Pueblo.

Zion's Lutheran Church in Trinidad

Trinidad—Zion's Lutheran Church

German-speaking Christians in Trinidad had no public worship services in German until a Lutheran pastor from Denver arrived in 1888. By September of 1889, the congregation had hired the architectural firm of Bulgar and Rapp, who also designed Temple Aaron and the First Baptist Church in Trinidad. The young, new Pastor Lothringer was away at a conference while the church council made plans for the laying of the cornerstone, and to include the participation of the local rabbi and his congregation. Lothringer vehemently opposed the plan, and when the council stuck to its guns about the proposed ecumenical event, he resigned. Pastor Kuns of Pueblo agreed to officiate, and so Trinidad's Jewish rabbi did indeed participate.

During a long succession of temporary pastors, changes were taking place. From 1912 on, services were conducted in English and German on alternating Sundays. In 1925, the church name was changed from German Evangelical Lutheran to Zion's Lutheran Church of Trinidad. Very soon its mission days were over, and it became a self-sustaining congregation. The church today is in excellent condition and a joy to behold.

Trinidad—Temple Aaron

Many of Colorado's mountain and plains towns of the late 1800s had small Jewish communities. Often there were just a few families who gathered for services in homes or temporary buildings. Few actual synagogues were built. Most worshipers went to Denver to the state's oldest and largest Jewish congregation, Temple Emanuel.

During the Rush to the Rockies era of gold fever in 1859, the mining town of Trinidad was founded about 20 miles north of what is now the New Mexico border. Early in Trinidad's history, Jewish businessmen and physicians arrived, many of them immi-

Temple Aaron in Trinidad

grants from Germany. There were enough Jews in Trinidad in 1871 to draw others from New Mexico for the observation of Rosh Hashanah. At the ceremonial circumcision of his son in 1883, Sam Jaffa suggested a fund drive to establish a temple. It was called Temple Aaron in honor of Jaffa's father, a German rabbi.

The Odd Fellows Hall and the Trinidad Opera House served as a gathering place for several years but by 1887, a building campaign was initiated. Two years later, under the watchful eye of architect Isaac Rapp, the red brick and pink sandstone synagogue with its distinctive and colorful onion-shaped dome was built. From Russia and eastern Europe, throughout Austria and southern Germany, the onion shape was common. Synagogues of the nineteenth century in America reflect the Jewish immigrants' fondness for that form.

Trinidad suffered a major coal strike in 1913–1914 and the town was agonizingly slow to recover. Many inhabitants left, including a large segment of the Jewish community. Rabbi Freudenthal led the congregation for 27 years. Following his death in 1916, no permanent rabbi was ever again engaged. Several generations of the Simon Sanders family took over leadership of the Jewish community. They continued to lead services well into the 1980s when a Sanders widow, Beatrice, kept the Temple operating.

In 1989, Temple Aaron's 100th birthday was celebrated, and the building was donated by the congregation to the Colorado Historical Society to be used as a museum—when and if there are no more Jews to worship there. So far, it continues as an operational synagogue and is an important landmark in Trinidad. It is the oldest continuously operating synagogue structure in the Rocky Mountain West.

THE SAN LUIS VALLEY

The San Luis Valley, 100 miles north to south and some 65 miles east to west, lies between the Sangre de Cristo Mountains and the San Juans. Its average altitude is over 7000 feet. Several American Indian tribes roamed the valley for thousands of years. Then, almost a century before the Pilgrims landed at Plymouth Rock, Spanish conquistadors explored the area and were soon followed by Spanish and Mexican settlers with their Catholic faith and Spanish language. The first permanent settlement in Colorado was San Luis, founded in 1851.

The valley, framed by its towering mountain boundaries, is home to precious examples of ancient Indian petroglyphs, numerous hot springs, and farmlands made fertile by a system of ditches held in common by its inhabitants. Scattered throughout the valley are missions and larger established churches, most reflecting Hispanic influences.

Our Lady of Guadalupe in Conejos, originally a tiny adobe church, is claimed to be the oldest Catholic congregation in the state. Founded in 1858, the parish served the Catholics of the entire San Luis Valley, and many of today's Catholic churches in the valley began as missions from this parish. The present building dates from the 1920s.

Begun in 1912, St. Joseph Catholic Church in Capulin took four years to complete. A commission, made up of parish men, provided manpower, horses and wagons to haul rock from the Hot Creek quarry some 10 miles distant from Capulin. Justo Duran from Monte Vista and Eugene Medina of Taos, New Mexico cut and worked the stone that was used in building today's church.

Christ the King Catholic Church in La Veta was built in 1946 of adobe blocks made from the earth in the church yard. Pueblo architect, Walter de Mordaunt, oversaw its construction. It is currently a mission of St. Mary Church in Walsenburg.

St. Joseph's Church in Capulin

Our Lady of Guadalupe in Conejos

St. Agnes Catholic Church in Saguache

Christ the King Church in La Veta

St. Francis of Assisi in Del Norte

Holy Family in Fort Garland

Blanca's Holy Family

Holy Name of Mary in Del Norte

San Acacio Viejo, said to be the oldest standing church in Colorado (1856)

San Francisco

St. Peter and Paul

Sangre de Cristo in San Luis

Los Fuertes

Alamosa—Sacred Heart Church

Getting a church and regular clergy for the Catholics in Alamosa was not so easy a century ago. Alamosa, Spanish for "full of cottonwoods," was a small agricultural settlement on the upper Rio Grande River in the heart of the valley. In the 1860s it was a mission served by Conejos, thirty miles to the south. During that time, Father Joseph Machebeuf used to make regular trips to assist the pastor at Conejos, and on these visits Father Machebeuf often said Mass at Alamosa, arriving in his familiar horse and buggy. He must have maintained an affection for the small devoted flock there; soon after he became Bishop of Denver in 1887, he arranged for the purchase of a lot in Alamosa for the group to build a church, and subsequently blessed the white frame structure himself.

The congregation soon began efforts to acquire a resident priest and parish status for their growing needs. Bishop Machebeuf died in 1889. His successor, Bishop Nicholas Matz, was not

Sacred Heart Church in Alamosa

prepared to accommodate the congregation's aspirations so readily, and transferred the mission to the jurisdiction of Holy Name of Mary Church in Del Norte. As for appointing a priest, Bishop Matz was sympathetic but not confident that the congregation could afford the additional expense, which would have amounted to $50 a month. A few years later a resident priest was assigned, but it was not until 1919 that Sacred Heart was designated a parish by Matz's successor, Bishop Tihen. By that time the original church had been enlarged and a new chapel, St. Rita's, dedicated.

In that same year, 1919, the thriving, confident parish and its new pastor, Father John Murphy, set their sights on a major building project. It would include a new church, school, rectory, and convent; Robert Willison, architect of the Denver Auditorium, was hired to design the complex.

As bazaar proceeds accrued and subscriptions were promised, St. Rita's was sold to the Lutherans and moved off the lot to make room for the new church when foundation work began in 1922. For the next six years, construction was intermittent as funds

United Presbyterian Church in Antonito

dried up. Members donated their own labor on occasion and were generous about digging even further into their pockets whenever an issue of quality came up, as it did in making the choice to use oak flooring. These were frustrating, heart-breaking years for the parish and for Father Murphy, whose health was weakened by the stress. He resigned in 1927 just a few months before the church was ready for use. The popular priest is credited with the vision, perseverance, and successful public relations that were required for several years to keep this enterprise in motion.

A weary but very proud and enthusiastic crowd of members, friends, and dignitaries participated in the dedication on a Sunday in May 1928. The well-wishers included Bishop Tihen and Governor "Billy" Adams. The parish's job was not over; for many years after the building was put into use, communicants were still contributing generously toward fixtures to complete and enhance the beauty of their church.

As early as the 1870s Presbyterian missionaries were active in the San Luis Valley. Mission schools and churches, as well as a Presbyterian college flourished. The Reverend Alexander Darley, brother of George Darley and a colleague of Sheldon Jackson, had an abiding interest in the culture of the Spanish-speaking people of the area; there were only two Anglo Presbyterian families in the area. The first of eight Spanish Presbyterian churches was inaugurated in 1876, and in 1877, the present location of the United Presbyterian Church of Antonito was secured and the church was built.

Monte Vista—First Presbyterian Church

Members of the Church of the Brethren were called "Dunkards," referring to their practice of baptism by triple immersion. In the late 1870s a group of Dunkards formed a congregation called Rock Creek Union Church in a community known as *Piedra Pintada* (Painted Rock) in the western part of the San Luis Valley. Meanwhile, those two intrepid Presbyterian preachers, George and Alexander Darley, came occasionally to hold worship services. In 1881, a petition signed by the "Rock Creek Ten"—a small company of the original Dunkards—requested the organization of a Presbyterian church. Soon a church building was begun. From eight miles away at Raton Creek, sandstone was hauled by wagons that each held about two tons. Each delivery took a day, including loading and unloading, traveling back and forth, and caring for the horses. Stonemason Robert Campbell joined the labor-intensive effort in 1898. Most of the carpenters involved were Swedish immigrants who ultimately became members of the congregation. In 1899, the sturdy First Presbyterian Church of Monte Vista was dedicated.

When the church was celebrating its 75th anniversary in 1956, Bernice Martin wrote *People of the Book,* a delightfully detailed record of the history of First Presbyterian. She said about the first pastor,

> An apocryphal tale about the Reverend Baum, undoubtedly exaggerated, claims that he locked the doors on Sunday and announced that the congregation would remain until all the money to finish the church was subscribed.

Later she added,

> The organ required a small boy sitting behind a screen to pump it, and sometimes the boy became inattentive and forgot to pump at critical moments, or actually went to sleep. The pay was 25 cents per Sunday. Many men still in the congregation remember their youthful experiences as boy pumper of that organ.

Monte Vista First Presbyterian Church

And in a charming human interest story involving the choir's lead soprano, Mrs. Martin wrote,

> The minister of the church had an incurable habit of running his sermon longer than the allotted time. Almost every week when he found he had talked too long he would cut the final hymn from the service.
>
> On this particular Sunday the seat fell out of Mrs. Edman's chair during the sermon and she slipped to the floor. Apparently not many had noticed what was happening so when fellow members of the choir attempted to help Mrs. Edman to her feet, she motioned them away. She continued sitting on the floor out of sight behind the choir rail, believing the minister would cut the last hymn as he usually did, and the service would be over in a few minutes. To her chagrin he did include the hymn, and announced, 'Stand up, Stand Up for Jesus.' The appropriateness of the song convulsed the choir, and after Mr. Edman [the choir director/organist] had played the introduction over several times Mrs. Edman scrambled to her feet to take her place as lead soprano. The choir sobered up enough to sing the hymn.

The Mormon Storehouse, or Stakehouse, in Manassa

The Mormons

Beginning in 1878, the Church of the Latter Day Saints established settlements in the San Luis Valley. Many Mormons heading westward to find places where they could practice their religion without controversy and unrest stopped in southern Colorado. They were assisted by Mormons from Salt Lake City who had arrived three decades earlier. By 1879, there were some 250 of the faithful in the valley. (In 1880 Mr. and Mrs. John Dempsey arrived in Manassa from Virginia. Their son, Jack, was to become the "Manassa Mauler" of boxing fame.)

In 1892, almost 2500 Mormons lived in several towns of the area. Manassa was the site of the regional bishop's office where the monthly prayer circle was held for 60 years beginning in 1913. The building, one of the few early Mormon structures that remain, is now called the Bishop's Storehouse. Today there are many modern, steepled Mormon churches throughout the San Luis Valley.

PLAINS

Calhan—St. Mary's Orthodox Church

Not all nineteenth century immigrants to the Rocky Mountain West chose the risky life of mining Colorado's store of precious minerals. Slovaks from Austro-Hungary with such names as Trojanovich, Manyik, Hlatki, and Pylypczuk, were homesteaders who brought with them their Orthodox heritage. By 1905, St. Mary's Orthodox church was built on a hill overlooking the high plains and the town of Calhan. Its builders came from Denver and stayed in the homes of area families while the church was under construction. Volunteers came from all the local denominations to assist in this labor of love.

In the early days, St. Mary's church school was well attended, and Slavonic chant rang out in the services. Soon, an additional Orthodox church was built in nearby Ramah. In 1927, a devastating fire destroyed the Calhan Church on the Hill. While one group of parishioners rebuilt the church, another group began to build on a new site. Eventually it became clear that the parish really only needed one church and efforts were focused on the new St. Mary's Church, which was completed and dedicated in 1932. By 1956, services were conducted in English, and the unaccompanied voices of the choir were singing the works of great Russian composers in four-part harmony.

St. Mary's Church is the repository of remembrances from all the Orthodox churches once active in the area. The carved tabernacle and Eternal Lamp are from the original Ramah church, and icons were gathered from Ramah and the old Church on the Hill to add to those at St. Mary's. A veritable jewel out on the plains, St. Mary's with its onion domes proclaims the still rich Orthodox traditions of her people.

St. Mary's Orthodox Church in Calhan

Virginia Dale Community Church (Photo by Jean Messinger)

Virginia Dale Community Church

Virginia Dale is a tiny speck on the map near the Wyoming state line, but the area is rich in history. Its very respectable-sounding name was given by Jack Slade, actually a notorious outlaw, who named it for his wife.

The church was built in 1879 on the Lilley Ranch by neighbors. In 1885, the building was moved five miles to "a more central location"—its present site on Highway 287 north of Fort Collins. The relocation was done at night by horse teams, perhaps the only time the busy ranchers could spare their time and equipment. The building was originally log construction; clapboard was added later.

The church's isolated, dramatic setting suggests the fortitude of its founders, an impression confirmed by a feeling that not a lot has changed for the church or for its supporters.

This doesn't mean the area lacked excitement in the early days. In 1862, Virginia Dale became a stop on the Overland Stage route west, and Jack Slade was made station master. Mr.

Slade didn't have the most respectable reputation to start with, and he was suspected of being a front for highwaymen active in the area who operated out of the legendary Robbers' Roost. He was dismissed in 1863, and in the following year was hanged by vigilantes in Montana.

The Volga Deutsch of the Plains

In the late eighteenth century, when German princess Catherine the Great became Czarina of All the Russias, she officially invited western Europeans to help develop the Volga Valley and southern steppes. Thousands of Germans, eager to escape political, religious and civil oppression, left their homeland and established colonies in Russia. Within a century, promises of civil rights began to erode. America beckoned with its wide open, western-frontier opportunities. The first immigrants arrived in Colorado in 1872, and the flow of families continued well into the twentieth century. Many came to farm or work in sugar-beet

Fort Morgan Zion Evangelical Lutheran Church

Fort Morgan Christ Congregational Church. Fort
Morgan was the destination of yet another group of
Volga Deutsch who founded a church called *Deutsche
Evangelische Christus Gemeinde* in 1907. By 1918 the Fort
Morgan city council had forbidden the use of the
German language—it was, of course, late World War I.
This hardship on the mostly German-speaking congre-
gation lasted only six weeks, but it is said to have begun
the tradition of displaying the American flag in church
sanctuaries. This white clapboard place of worship has
survived as a much-loved and much-cared-for church.

factories. Because these newcomers shared a common religion
and language, they tended to stick together in settlements where
neighbors could easily support each other. They often built
churches while members still lived in dirt-floored dugouts or
shacks. These churches remain as reminders of earlier, hardy
frontier people who kept their priorities in line in the face of almost unbelievable challenges. Today, some of their descendants
own and work the big high-plains ranches in eastern Colorado.

Platteville - St. John's Evangelical Lutheran Church. Some of the Volga Deutsch immigrants to eastern Colorado founded a Lutheran church in Evans. In 1925, it was moved a few miles south to Platteville. Services were conducted in German until 1938 when English became the regular language. The original bell still announces the beginning and end of each service. (Photo by Jean Messinger)

Immanuel Lutheran Church in Bethune

Bethune—Immanuel Lutheran Church

In the late 1880s, Germans who had been living in Czarist Russia emigrated to the United States. Some of them settled in Colorado, attracted to the plains that reminded them of the steppes of their adopted homeland. The community they founded near Bethune was called *Friedensfeld,* meaning field of peace. It soon became known as "The Settlement," a name that remains although the area is now all but deserted. In 1893, the German pioneers built a limestone church. Each family donated eight wagon-loads of rock from nearby rivers. By the 1920s a larger church was clearly called for, and once again labor was supplied by members of the congregation. Today's Immanuel Lutheran sits proudly on a hill, having survived blizzards, tornadoes, hailstorms, dust storms, prairie fires, droughts, and grasshopper plagues—a true example of "faith in high places."

Windsor—St. John's Evangelical Lutheran

The spiritual inheritance of the congregation of St. John's Evangelican Lutheran Church is indeed a tribute to great faith. The story begins along the Volga River in Russia around the turn of the century. German colonies had long flourished there but the threat of compulsory service in the Czar's armies drove them to seek refuge elsewhere. Meanwhile the Great Western Sugar Company in Windsor was soliciting workers to process sugar beets, an important industry in the area. Some of the Russian Germans immigrated to the little towns of eastern Colorado. They brought their strong religious faith and of course, their

St. John's Evangelical Lutheran Church in Windsor

German, Russian-peppered language. Before the turn of the century, the first families arrived in Windsor, followed almost immediately by others.

The little congregation of St. John's held worship services in a small rented building until 1906 when a proper church was built. A tower and north wing were added, and then three bells were placed in the tower. When tolled for a funeral, the biggest bell signified an elderly person, the medium one was for the middle-aged, and the sound of the smallest was for a child—a sort of "Papa, Mama and Baby bell" application.

Throughout the years, German was the language of both Sunday school and services but by the 1940s, English was spoken along with German. A photograph taken in 1912 shows that St. John's looks very much as it did then.

Prairie View Church. Although it was built as a schoolhouse in 1907, the Prairie View building near Pawnee National Grassland figured in high-plains history as a multi-purpose center. During the homesteading days, small rural schools were built every few miles. Later all but the one at Prairie View were consolidated into regional schools. During the 1930s and 1940s Reverend Gertrude Horn served in the same role as her male predecessors, the early circuit riders. The Prairie View center has been home to potluck suppers, cowboy dances, Sunday school and church services. It stands alone out on the plains, a compelling reminder of the remote settlements of turn-of-the-century homesteaders. (Photo by Jean Messinger)

Platteville—First United Methodist Church

A one-room frame building thirty-by-fifty-feet, was dedicated in 1882 as the First Methodist Episcopal Church of Platteville. When a new church was needed in 1919, a complicated plan was put into action. The old church was moved from its foundation and a larger basement area was dug. Then the little church was moved back onto the new foundation because funds for a bigger church were not yet available. It wasn't until 1929 that the old frame building was once again removed from its base and a new church was built. It became the First United Methodist Church.

This congregation, obviously not short of innovative ideas, came up with another one in 1951; a project called "God's Little Acre" enabled the congregation to build a parsonage. "God's Little Acre" encouraged each family to donate the money from the sale of an acre's worth of produce or a farm animal to the building fund. Once again this farming community answered the call, a characteristic of many small towns of rural Colorado.

Platteville's First United Methodist Church

First Congregational Church in Eaton

Ault First Christian Church, Disciples of Christ (Photo by Jean Messinger)

Ault—First Christian Church, Disciples of Christ

Because of its soft, neutral colors and shady location, this tidy, pleasing structure is not one that attracts immediate attention. Nor does it look as old as it is. Indeed it takes a second look to realize the building is a house of worship, and that it has always been Ault's First Christian Church. Its small scale and lack of obvious ecclesiastical features give it an almost domestic look. The explanation for its appearance might be found in its beginnings.

Ault is a small town on the railroad running from Cheyenne to Greeley. In 1903 a group of women from Ault and farm wives from the surrounding area organized a Dorcas Society. (Dorcas was an early Christian disciple who was "completely occupied with good deeds and almsgiving." - Acts 9:36.) The purpose and activities of the Society were consistent with social gatherings of rural women at the turn of the century; that is, valued fellowship time spent in Bible study, quilting, bake sales, and serving home-cooked church suppers. The ladies, about 15 in all, met in each others' homes. When a meeting was scheduled for the country, the hostess's farmer husband would hitch up his wagon, load straw and blankets in the back, settle his small children on the seat beside him, and make "taxi" rounds picking up the guests. The ride was accompanied by much chatter, laughing and even singing; the driver may or may not have considered his task a welcome relief from regular chores.

These ladies, their husbands and families no doubt became a compatible, close-knit group, and in three years they determined to build their own church. Mrs. Carrie Hasbrock, the Society's first president, designed the building; and on Christmas Day 1906 construction began. It must have been a mild winter because the first services were held in the new church on February 3, 1907, barely 40 days later.

This was an unusual group, dedicated to their purpose and apparently of many talents. Men and women alike did the actual construction and supervision. The interior is well appointed and as charming as the exterior. The structure itself can be considered vernacular in the purest and most positive interpretation of the term.

Rankin Presbyterian Church in Brush

Brush—Rankin Presbyterian Church

Under the direction of the Home Mission Board and the Central Presbyterian Church of Denver, a young cowboy set out eastward on horseback from Denver to the newly incorporated town of Brush. The year was 1886 and the cowboy, Hugh W. Rankin, was an evangelist. He held services in a private home and urged the community to form a church. The first organizational meeting was held in the schoolhouse, and a decision was made to name the proposed church for the courageous cowboy who had first inspired them. It took 150,000 locally-made, red bricks to erect the English Gothic Revival building. A photo taken in 1907 reveals that the church is substantially unchanged today. The brick walls have been carefully repointed, and protective coverings have been installed on the stained-glass windows, all of which has kept the old church looking new. It is the oldest church building in the high plains town of Brush.

Julesburg's Seventh-day Adventist Church

Julesburg—Seventh-day Adventist Church

This building with its intriguing entrance treatment started as a Methodist church. It was built in 1906 to replace a frame church that burned the year before. The old structure was very attractive, with Carpenter Gothic detailing and a unique and handsome tower—an element often well-treated on historic Methodist churches of Colorado. Concerning the new church, its brick construction indicates both financial means and seriousness on the part of the congregation that built it. When the Methodists moved to a larger, new building in 1952, this church became home to Julesburg's newly organized Seventh-day Adventists.

The collective settlements named Julesburg were important stops on the routes west. They were strategically located on the wagon trails and Union Pacific Railway Line at the junction of the North and South Platte Rivers. French fur traders, Mormons, missionary Father deSmet, and many others passed through on their way to California, Wyoming, Utah, Oregon, or into Colorado. Jules Beni established a trading post in the 1850s, and Fort

Sedgwick was erected nearby in 1864. As a consequence, area history is as varied and exciting as any in Colorado.

Seldom was there a place on the frontier that didn't attract people of faith. Despite its reputation for riotous living, in Julesburg there were believers who arranged meetings and erected churches. The present town, Julesburg number four, was incorporated in 1886, and a Methodist congregation was organized that same year.

Highland Lake Church (Highlandlake)

Highland Lake Church (Highlandlake)

Readers won't instantly recognize the Highland Lake Church from its modified appearance in the 1990 Bruce Willis movie, *Die Hard II.* On the other hand, anyone who watched the film will be relieved to see that flames and gunfire did not lay waste to the historic structure, and its stained-glass windows were not blown out but are actually in better condition than they were when filming began. The graphic destruction seen on the screen was the product of special effects technology. Arrangements to use the building netted the church a new roof, a paint job and repairs, as well as restoration of the leaded, memorial windows.

An early settler, L. C. "Deacon" Mead, named his homestead Highlandlake from Sir Walter Scott's *Lady of the Lake;* there was nearby a small, spring-fed lake which had been a buffalo wallow. Subsequently a dike at the lake enlarged it for irrigation as well as recreation purposes.

When the Meads came to the area in 1871, the closest church was in Longmont. Seven miles by horse and buggy each Sunday was a substantial undertaking for farmers in those days; Deacon Mead made the trip regularly on one of his gray mules. In 1881, he helped to organize a Congregational church for the growing settlement at Highlandlake.

Another important founder and homesteader was George Davis, a zealous Congregational minister from Massachusetts who established churches at Central City, Blackhawk, and Longmont before he settled with his family in Highlandlake in 1879. Later the church bought the Davis home for a parsonage, even before the church was erected.

It was 1896 before the congregation was able to build a church, on a lot donated by Deacon Mead. Their pastor, Miss Mary Bumstead from Roxbury, Massachusetts, was instrumental in encouraging the endeavor, and she personally raised funds back east for construction. The large front window was a gift from the YMCA of Naugatuck, Connecticut.

During the following years, the Great Western Sugar Company built a railroad spur to the area to pick up sugar beets, but the line just missed Highlandlake. As a result, business in the town declined, church membership dwindled, and so did support for the pretty white church at the edge of the lake. By 1917, no longer able to pay a minister, the church ceased to function. The remaining, loyal residents entered into an agreement with the Congregational Church to keep the building intact and under local control. It was thus agreed that the community would elect a board to maintain the premises and hold a meeting at least once a year. For failure to comply, local authority over the building would be relinquished, and the church's fate would be in the hands of out-of-town authorities.   ·

By 1921 the first of the required annual meetings took place, and since then a picnic reunion each summer brings together friends, neighbors, and supporters of the church's independence. And people will no doubt talk for a long time about the boost that came from Hollywood.

The Brethren Church and town of Hygiene remain but the sanitorium is long gone. The unusual name is a reference to Hygeia, ancient Greek goddess of health. (Photo by Jean Messinger)

Hygiene—Church of the Brethren

A place with the intriguing name of Hygiene is likely to have an intriguing story to match, and this one surely does.

Church of the Brethren is a Protestant denomination formerly called German Baptist. The sect is also known as "Dunkard" because of its practice of baptism by triple immersion. The sect originated in 1708 with a small group of dissenters in Germany. Persecution there forced the founder Alexander Mack and his followers to resettle in Germantown, Pennsylvania at the invitation of William Penn. The Germantown church is considered the Mother Church of the Brethren.

Descendents of a group of Brethren who later settled in Pella, Iowa came to Colorado's St. Vrain Valley in the 1870s. They were farmers and merchants who formed a small community near Longmont which they named Pella; it no longer exists. They continued their religious meetings by gathering in each other's cabins, and in 1877 one of their number, the Reverend J. S. Flory, organized a church.

The present stone structure dates from 1880 and is the oldest Brethren church in Colorado. Parishioners brought the stone from Lyons and erected a building that bears resemblance to the Mother Church in Germantown. They did the construction work themselves; even the benches and floorboards were hand-planed.

The Dunkard settlers did not stay long in the Valley, and by 1907 regular services in the little church were discontinued. Pastor Flory stayed behind with his family and moved up the road a bit to begin a new community around the sanitorium he built for tubercular patients. He named his new enterprise Hygiene.

It was not uncommon to find a Brethren pastor also functioning as a businessman. Brethren rules wouldn't allow their ministers to be compensated for their work in the church, although that is no longer true. (One Brethren pastor was excommunicated when he accepted remuneration for preaching to Mennonites!)

Ryssby. Travelers along a country road northeast of Boulder are surprised to see this touch of old-world charm, a picturesque reminder of Swedish migration to Colorado during the late nineteenth century.

Ryssby Church

The account of Swedish immigration into Boulder County in the 1860s is one of courage, determination, hardship, disappointment, and occasional reward. In a land that challenged and broke hearts but not spirits, the newcomers persisted and carved out new lives on terms laid down by the Western frontier. In 1869 a group of seven families formed the first Swedish settlement in Colorado. They came chiefly from the parish of Ryssby in the Swedish province of Smaland, a land of poor soil and hardworking people.

In Colorado the daily struggle to survive occupied the settlers for the first few years. Leader Sven Johnson's home was the only frame house in the colony and served as community center. Here they celebrated in the old ways: weddings, Midsummer Day, Reformation Day, and Christmas. Those special social and religious occasions gave them moral support and helped the immigrants retain their heritage from the old country.

By 1873 there were 14 families in the Ryssby settlement, and two years later a schoolhouse was built on land donated by Sven Johnson. With a bona fide gathering place, regular religious services could be held.

In 1877 a young pastor, Fred Lagerman, joined the colony from Augustana College in Illinois. He soon organized a congregation which resolved to build a church. He left, however, and during planning and construction the congregation was without a minister most of the time. Hugo Anderson gave three acres, parishioners quarried stone from August Olander's homestead nearby, and the $50 Abraham Anderson gave to insure his burial in the churchyard was applied toward building a fence around the churchyard. By 1882 the building was ready, and not surprisingly it resembled the mother church back in Sweden.

Soon there were 50 families in the Ryssby community as hard times in Sweden brought more immigrants to Colorado; by 1890 there were 10,000 Swedes in the state. However, the 1893 nationwide depression in the U.S. as well as agricultural problems began to force local farmers to leave the area. By 1905 there weren't enough families to sustain the Ryssby Church, and it stood empty for nine years. In 1914 the remaining members merged with Elim congregation in Longmont. First Evangelical Lutheran Church of Longmont has absorbed Elim and now owns the Ryssby Church.

Ryssby is no longer used for regular Sunday services, but since 1924 Midsummer Day services have been held in an attempt to preserve some of Ryssby's legacy—in Sweden and in Colorado. Traditional December candlelight services are another part of annual celebrations. During the 1960s, descendants of the pioneers expended a great deal of effort and resources to renovate and restore the old church and its cemetery. The interior was extensively redone as well, and its sparkling, white interior makes a romantic setting for weddings.

The name Buckhorn Presbyterian Church comes from Masonville's location in the Buckhorn Valley, southeast of Fort Collins. The area is prime deer habitat, and provides them a diet of buckbrush when snow covers the ground. Early settlers found an accumulation of antlers scattered over the area—hence the name "Buckhorn."

Masonville—Buckhorn Presbyterian Church

The Masonville Buckhorn Presbyterian Church was built in 1911 on an acre purchased for $50, plus other donated land. Local builders used stone from a member's quarry less than a mile away.

Herbert Spence's father was a charter member of this church, and Herbert is now the only communicant from that original congregation. He recalls that during World War II a strong wind toppled the church steeple; as we have seen, nature can be hard on high country churches. The young men of the community were away in service, and the senior Spence and one other man were about the only adult men remaining. Building materials as well as labor were in short supply, so the two men boarded up the base where the steeple had been and covered it with roll roofing. It was several years before the present, modified steeple was erected.

During the 1960s a benefactress and member named Clara Skelly donated $10,000 to modernize and enlarge the church. When costs exceeded that amount she gave more until the project was finished. Ironically, the night before the dedication of Skelly Hall to honor her, she passed away quite suddenly.

Timnath Presbyterian Church

Timnath Presbyterian Church is the only church this small community has ever had. It was built by members of the congregation in 1888. A parsonage was built for Pastor Charles Taylor before the church was, and since he was also the postmaster, his kitchen in the new manse was the post office. It was Postmaster Reverend Taylor who named the town, and his inspiration came from the Old Testament: Samson had associations with a town called Timnath.

The church building looked quite different then, wearing a red brick exterior. Its present white stucco surface was applied in

Timnath Presbyterian Church

the 1950s in order to preserve the brick. The original windows were ruby red or blue glass with a delicate etched fern leaf pattern, made in Bavaria especially for the Timnath church. In 1946 those windows were removed and replaced by plain, gold-colored glass, probably with the honest intention of giving the church a more up-to-date look.

More recently, stunning new leaded glass windows have become the *pièce de résistance* of this tidy, unpretentious church on the prairie east of Fort Collins. The story of their creation and of their creator is so heartwarming as to be almost anachronistic in this era of TV evangelism.

Like Sheldon Jackson before him, the Reverend Paul Moyer answered a call to Alaska. In 1957, as a young pastor from Pennsylvania, he took his bride Mary Ellen and made a gigantic cultural leap to serve a Haida Indian village of 150 on an island off the coast of Alaska. Another assignment took the Moyers to Barrow, at the edge of the Arctic Ocean, and to Palmer before returning to the lower 48. They spent the following ten years in Lingle, Wyoming before coming to the Timnath church in 1976.

While getting acquainted with the premises, Paul Moyer discovered a few pieces of beautiful old glass stored in an old shed behind the church. It was determined that the glass was from the original windows removed during the remodeling after World War II. To rework this antique glass back into the existing windows would have been too costly, and so the pastor, intrepid and unwavering in all things, undertook to design and make new windows himself. This initial project resulted in replacing the two windows on either side of the main entrance.

With the congregation's support and extra money coming forth from donations for memorials, Moyer eventually created new windows for the entire church. Although the windows are modern in concept and design, they are still very appropriate to their setting in a simple structure that is more than 100 years old. Their images represent things that are important personally to Moyer and to the congregation, but at the same time they reflect traditional Christian symbolism.

The complexity of such an undertaking required a high level of imagination and artistry. The Reverend Moyer may have been an inexperienced craftsman when he began, but these striking leaded-glass windows are hardly the work of an amateur. When the pastor retired from Timnath Presbyterian Church in 1990, he left a visible legacy that will be in place as long as the church stands.

Canon City—United Presbyterian Church

If it is true that one can tell a lot about a community by the number, variety, and condition of its churches, Canon City reads easily and accurately. The United Presbyterian Church is only one of several outstanding historic churches in this town better known for the famous Royal Gorge Park on the Arkansas River, as well as the state and territorial penitentiaries.

The building was designed by Canon City architect C. C. Rittenhouse and was dedicated in 1902. Its style is eclectic in that it combines elements of Richardsonian Romanesque in the main body with eyecatching, highly-decorated treatment of its Queen

United Presbyterian Church in Canon City

Anne tower. Local quarries provided the stone, which was laid by Korvel & Sell; they were local stonecutters, natives of Germany, who did a considerable amount of work in the area.

The bell in the tower was a feature of an earlier church, and it was formerly installed in a separate, ground-level structure because the original small frame church couldn't support it. The fire department was nearby, and so for 20 years until the new church was built, the bell was also used as the fire alarm. Menealy Bell Foundry of Troy, New York made the bell; its donor was a New York woman who preferred to keep her address and her reasons for the gift private.

To enter the sanctuary of this church is to be nearly overwhelmed by the beautiful windows. They were made Tiffany-style with tiny, multiple facets of colored glass. One reproduces Plockhorst's "Jesus and the Children," and the other "The Good Sheperd."

The present congregation of the United Presbyterian Church is the result of a union of three separate groups of local Presbyterians, who wisely chose this imposing structure as their common house of worship.

Canon City—Christ Episcopal Church

The 1902 Christ Episcopal Church of Canon City is a sophisticated version of English Gothic adapted by one who knew his trade—Thomas MacLaren. He was a highly respected Colorado Springs architect whose career there extended from his arrival in 1894 until his death in 1929. The Scottish MacLaren came from academic technical training, which was not common preparation for American architects before the turn of the century. He was at his best as an eclectic interpreter—eclectic in the sense of borrowed inspiration. His buildings were stylistically consistent, however, not the mixture of elements eclecticism often produced in America. Thomas MacLaren's impressive architectural legacy includes monumental public buildings, churches, schools, and residences. He was particularly competent designing in the Classical, English Gothic, and Spanish Revival styles.

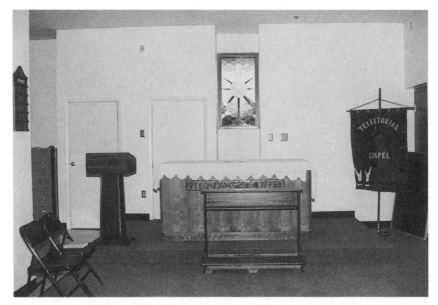

The chapel at the Territorial Prison in Canon City

Canon City—"Old Max" Territorial Prison Chapel

Since the Colorado State Legislature cannot fund prison chapels, religious and counseling services once took place in a room that is now the warden's office. In 1987 a small vacant room in the former infirmary of the pre-statehood prison became the chapel. It was supported by money and work donated by inmates, outside churches, businesses, and visiting clergymen. Inmate craftsmen designed and made furniture, windows, and banners that add a religious environment for the multi-faith services held there.

Inmate-designed window

Holy Cross Abbey in Canon City

Canon City—Holy Cross Abbey

The oldest religious order in Roman Catholicism is the Order of St. Benedict, dating from the sixth century. Its members are commonly called Benedictines. Two of the order's monks from Pennsylvania arrived in Colorado in 1886 at the invitation of Bishop Machebeuf, who needed priests in Breckenridge. There they founded St. Mary's Church.

Soon more Benedictines came to the state, and some eventually settled in Canon City where a priory was formed. A pioneer apple-orchard entrepreneur, Benjamin Rockafellow, donated a 220-acre parcel of land known as "Fruitmore" for a church. In 1925 that church was elevated to Holy Cross Abbey and housed a growing number of monks who served in surrounding parishes, supplied four chaplaincies, ran a boys' summer camp, and administered the Abbey School. Accordingly, several buildings were added to the site.

By the late 1980s the school and camp closed, and many ancillary buildings were rented out or leased. But the Abbey itself, a grand building housing the chapel and monastic residence, is still the home of a group of Benedictine monks.

The United Methodist Church of Cheyenne Wells uses buttresses in an unusual way: on the principal facade.

Cheyenne Wells—United Methodist Church

In a town whose name is a reminder of earlier, native American occupants of its site, the Methodist Episcopal Church claims to be the first Protestant church organized (1885) in eastern Colorado. Father Dyer came to preach at Hugo, and Cheyenne Wells was on the Hugo circuit. One look at the Colorado map shows a lot of prairie and not much in between for nearly seventy miles from Hugo to Cheyenne Wells—quite a challenge for a circuit rider in the 1880s.

The present church was erected in 1922, and it replaced a smaller, white frame structure. The overall design of this well-maintained church is eclectic. Old theatre seats were installed as pews in the new church, an economical strategy and not an uncommon seating solution. The basement was intended to double as gymnasium for the high school basketball team.

Bemis-Taylor Chapel in Black Forest

Black Forest—Bemis-Taylor Chapel

Alice Bemis Taylor is best known as a patron of the arts and Colorado Springs' influential benefactor. She grew up in that city, the daughter of Judson Bemis who owned Bemis Paper Bag Company in St. Louis. In 1903 Alice married Frederick Taylor, and they, too, lived in Colorado Springs.

Mr. Taylor died in 1927. Soon after, his widow began building a retreat complex which she called La Forêt (The Forest) on wooded land in the Black Forest, 16 miles northeast of Colorado Springs. In addition to her own summer home, there were cabins and accommodations for servants and guests. It is surprising to note that in its small-town days prior to World War II, Colorado Springs' wealthy residents as well as out-of-staters sometimes had summer cabins in the canyons, foothills, and unspoiled areas not far from town.

Mrs. Taylor was especially interested in traditional art of the Southwest and traveled to New Mexico on several occasions, collecting. It was on one of these trips that she met a young architect, John Gaw Meem. She engaged Meem's services, and in 1929 the chapel was built at La Forêt as a memorial to her husband.

Meem had come west as a young man to recuperate, as so many did, from tuberculosis. Trained as an engineer, he never finished formal architectural schooling but studied and worked under Isaac Hamilton Rapp in Rapp's architectural firm in Santa Fe. Meem later had his own practice and received further patronage from Mrs. Taylor. He designed her great gift to Colorado Springs, the Fine Arts Center, built in 1936. He married Mrs. Taylor's niece, Faith Bemis, who was herself an architect.

When Meem accepted the commission for the Taylor chapel,

The chapel icons by Santa Fe artist Eugenie Shonnard are traditionally Catholic; however, their artistic appeal is as universal as the adobe exterior.

he had not yet designed a traditional church in the adobe style. His mentor, Isaac Rapp, endorsed the use of pueblo-style architecture as seen in Santa Fe's famous La Fonda Hotel, which Meem also worked on. Adobe is a very old, indigenous material and vernacular style in New Mexico; at this time it had quite specific revival applications. In the natural, isolated setting of La Forêt, the style was appropriate for Mrs. Taylor's small family chapel.

John Gaw Meem went on to use the pueblo style successfully in later works. He became an advocate for preserving the unique heritage of New Mexico by continuing to apply it to his own architectural projects with originality and practicality. The chapel he designed for Mrs. Taylor served that purpose, and it stands as a memorial to both Taylors and to Meem himself—purposeful, unpretentious, and enduring. Meem's long career was one of distinction not only in design but in endeavors relating to preservation, restoration, and planning. He died in 1983 at the age of 89.

In 1944 the Bemis Taylor Foundation donated La Forêt to the Colorado Congregational Conference, which proceeded to modernize and expand the facilities for use as a religious retreat camp for adults and children. It is presently used by various groups for meetings, conferences, training events, educational and Elderhostel sessions, and reunions. The chapel is often used for weddings.

Christ Episcopal Church in Castle Rock. Its entrance was on the long side at the southwest corner (left side). With subsequent remodeling, the door has been replaced by a window that matches the other two on that wall.

Castle Rock—Christ Episcopal Church

The two stone churches in Castle Rock were quite similar in appearance in their original forms. The older of the two, St. Francis of Assisi, was built by Catholics in 1888. It was the first church building in Castle Rock. Local tradition claims that early day circuit-rider priests who came to say Mass relied on the security of a hidden pistol. It isn't recorded if only priests were in such danger, but history does indicate that cash collections were not large among the faithful of any denomination. The congregation abandoned this church in 1966, and it remained vacant until 1975 when it was converted into a popular eating establishment. The integrity of its historic interior has been surprisingly well preserved, which gives it a charming and distinctive ambiance for dining.

Although Castle Rock didn't become a town until 1881, Episcopal services are recorded from 1875. A congregation was first organized in 1905 by English and Welsh miners and farmers who wanted to continue their familiar Anglican affiliation. They built Christ Episcopal Church at Fourth and Lewis in 1907. Assistance by pastors out of Littleton, Sedalia, and Denver continued for many years.

In Britain, stone is historically the most common building material. With quarries being worked near Castle Rock, stone for Christ Church construction was another way of extending the British tradition into Douglas County. Both St. Francis of Assisi and Christ Church used local rhyolite, which is a fine-grained volcanic rock similar to granite and usually exhibits flow lines. The original silhouette of each church was a small gabled rectangle, the type seen in several of the historic Episcopal stone churches throughout Colorado.

The parish continued its mission status; membership remained small for many years and naturally money was scarce. Some touching testimony survives that illustrates the responsibility and loyalty this congregation felt toward its ministry. For example, the accounting in 1909 records shows total expenditures of $427; more than ten percent of that amount was passed on to various missions. While the church's guild women were raising money in bits to pay for the new church by sponsoring dances, and serving community dinners and oyster suppers, they were also supporting the Episcopal hospital in Denver. In fact, nearly one-third of the church's income came from the guild. Before the church was built, these money-raising events had to be held in a borrowed hall where there was no running water.

Self-sustaining parish status was achieved in 1957, but the added financial burden of independence has not diminished Christ Church's commitment to its missions. It budgets fifty percent of its resources for outreach as it continues to serve an impressive number of community agencies for social needs.

St. Philip-in-the-Field Episcopal, Sedalia

Sedalia—St. Philip-in-the-Field Episcopal

When Bishop Spaulding consecrated Bear Canon Church in 1889, he renamed it St. Philip-in-the-Field because he was reminded of St. Philip meeting the Ethiopian eunuch in the desert as described in the Book of Acts.

This congregation has been active since 1870, and the church construction date is listed as 1872. However, completion of construction was delayed for several years because a man posing as an itinerant minister helped to raise $600 for that purpose, then disappeared along with the money. The disheartened congregation was slow to accomplish their goal a second time.

Sixth-generation descendants of the founders of St. Philip's are currently attending services here. Both the church and its historic Bear Canon Cemetery, also established in 1870, were placed on the National Register of Historic Landmarks in 1971.

St. Mark Presbyterian Church in Elbert (Photo by Jean Messinger)

Elbert—St. Mark Presbyterian Church (USA)

The town and county were named in honor of Sam Elbert, Colorado territorial governor in 1873–1874. St. Mark Presbyterian Church was the first Protestant church in Elbert County. It was constructed in 1889 by Taylor Green with help, as usual, from the community. Mr. Green was a local carpenter, Justice of the Peace, and an elder of St. Mark's. The pews he made for the sanctuary are still in use.

The original structure had no tower. When a bell was donated in 1940, it was mounted directly over the auditorium. But the building shook so much when the bell was rung that a separate tower and belfry had to be added to house the bell. That modification also added considerable interest to the front of the church.

Some of the smallest places contribute the most dramatic stories to the narrative about Colorado churches. In May 1935, a devastating flooding of Kiowa Creek washed away or damaged over 60 homes in Elbert. Many businesses as well as the railroad lines into town were also destroyed. Because the Elbert church was on high ground it was untouched and was able to be used as a refuge center for the area. In addition to relief work by the Red Cross on the premises, the *Denver Post* sponsored food drops from a plane flying in and out of Denver.

The town never fully recovered from that disaster, but the church has survived. After minor changes of name and affiliations throughout its existence, it is now St. Mark Presbyterian Church (USA), and in 1980 the building was rightly placed on the National Register of Historic Places.

Ruth Memorial Chapel in Parker

Parker—Ruth Memorial Chapel

Until Denver's mushroom growth during the last quarter of the twentieth century, Parker was a separate, small rural community 15 miles to the south between Denver and Castle Rock. Suburbia has since blurred the metropolitan boundaries, but picturesque commercial facades of distinctly nineteenth-century vintage verify the community's pre-Baby Boomer existence. Pine Grove was the town's name in those days. It was renamed for the postmaster James Parker and his brother George, when the railroad came to town in 1882.

Religious services were held for many years in the village schoolhouse, which still stands nearby. One of the circuit riders who came through the area on monthly visits was Father Dyer, who no doubt ministered to all denominations. One Parker resident, Dr. Heath, was a longtime and persistent advocate for a church for Parker, and he donated land and money for the building. The community did the rest and the structure was completed in 1913.

From the church's own history, this description by Gertrude
Lewis Davidson must have been repeated many times for each
homemade, cooperative church construction project. She relates:

> There were not too many people in the town of Parker and
> many of the farmers who wanted to help had very little time by
> the time they did the milking and morning chores then drove the
> team to Parker it wasn't too long till it was time for them to start
> for home to do chores and milking . . . my father took a team and
> scraper to help with the digging the basement—that was a nine
> mile trip each day for him. (sic)

Mrs. Davidson's parents gave the first Bible to the church
when it was dedicated in May of 1913, in memory of their two-
year-old son who had drowned the year before. The Bible was
bought with money from the little boy's bank.

The church's roster of ministers lists a different one nearly
every year or two until the early 1970s. Yet they each left their
mark, and some charming stories are told about these pastors
who touched lives in Parker so briefly. The Reverend J. P. Varner,
who preached in the old schoolhouse, was given a pillow by a
thoughtful parishioner—to kneel on so his trousers wouldn't get
dirty. For those who wished baptism by immersion, Varner ac-
commodated them in a pond on his ranch; it was always an occasion for picnicking and an outing in the country.

The only lady pastor came, not surprisingly, during wartime
1943. Miss Lucy Sands is described as a "gracious and lovely
young woman." Another wartime personality was the Reverend
Jenkinson, who was English and described as " . . . something
else again." At any rate, his brief tenure left an imprint. A widower with three children, he no doubt had his hands full and apparently had little skill or patience with the coal stove used to
heat the church. The narrative continues, "Mr. Jenkinson was a
well-educated man and was in the process of translating the Bible
into Sanskrit but he didn't know how to make a fire." One winter
night he fled the parsonage crying out, "They're bombing the
mawnse!" It was instead some mischievous boys throwing snow-
balls against the house.

Continued growth in northeast Douglas County was accompanied by growth in the Parker Methodist church, which prompted reorganization and expansion of its facilities. In 1980 a new, much larger sanctuary was built. Ruth Memorial Chapel was extensively renovated in 1988 in preparation for the church's 75th anniversary, and it is used now as adjunct space for Sunday school, weddings, receptions, etc. Its significance now affirmed by National Register status, the chapel's simple, sturdy lines are a continuation of what Parker used to be.

La Junta, St. Andrew's Episcopal Church. Its architect was Thomas MacLaren, who also designed Christ Episcopal Church in Canon City.

First Christian Church in Holly

RECYCLED CHURCHES

Loveland—Private Residence/Artists' Studio

The spatial organization and interior dimensions of churches lend themselves to a variety of adaptive reuse situations. This attractive property blends so well into its residential neighborhood that the building's original purpose does not stand out to a casual passerby. It formerly served the parish of St. John's Catholic Church in Loveland, but has not been used as a house of worship for many years. Its history includes several alternative uses, vacancy and deterioration, condemnation, renovation for office space and then for combined residence and private studio. The 30-foot, barrel-vaulted ceiling and north light provide favorable living/work environment for the painters who occupy it. The church was built in 1901 and the high-quality brick used for the exterior is in very good condition. Some of the original stained glass remains on the facade.

There are other, as the English say, "redundant" churches in Loveland that have also been converted by artists. This one in particular has been domesticated benignly, with little if any apparent modification to the exterior. The result is a tasteful, well-tended and unique neighbor, and fortunately for Loveland, a preserved and visible piece of the town's heritage.

168

Private residence/artists' studio in Loveland

The charmingly-named Angels in the Attic Gift Shop in Monument occupies the building that was once the original St. Peter's Catholic Church, founded in 1911. The parish now occupies a large new church.

Bailey—Witch's Hat. Eclectic may be too weak a word for the home of Steve and Marlene Hare in the mountain town of Bailey. According to the Hares it was originally a Mennonite church. At some point in its history, the two-story log structure acquired an eye-catching, dark, wooden steeple, giving the building its local name of "witch's hat." Over the years, a wild variety of owners and renters, mostly artists and craftspeople, added levels and details resulting in an almost unbelievable architectural conglomeration. The Hares have given the house their own decorative touches, so that one's first and lasting impression is that here is a much-loved and certainly unique home.

Noah's Ark Children's Center in La Jara

Las Animas—Troll Haus Restaurant. Episcopalian Bishop John F. Spaulding consecrated the Church of the Messiah in the Arkansas Valley town of Las Animas in 1888. Its next life was that of an art gallery in 1976. Finally in 1984, a kitchen was added and it soon opened as the Troll Haus Restaurant. A few pews and the original stained-glass windows as well as a piece of the altar rail remain to remind diners of the building's religious origins.

The Ordway Senior Citizens Center began as the town's Methodist church in 1904. The first donation of $25.00 is said to have come from an auction. It seems a message arrived during a church social announcing Grover Cleveland's election as President of the United States. The highest bid for the message itself was paid by a Mr. Kent of Buffalo, New York. He gave the money to the church building fund.

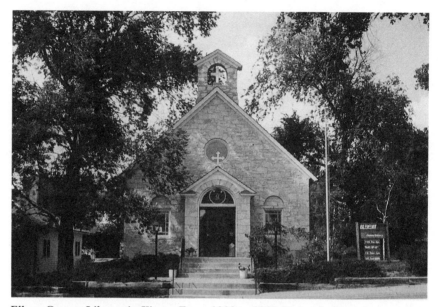

Elbert County Library in Kiowa. From 1903 to 1968 St. Ann's Church, a vernacular building with steep gabled roof and arched windows and door, served local Catholic families. Built with help from parishioners and other volunteers, its construction was supervised by Father Eusebius Schlingman, O.S.B.. The stone, which came from a nearby quarry, was hand-cut and hauled to Kiowa by mule train. Today it is cherished and cared for as the county library. (credit: Jean Messinger)

Foothills Art Center in Golden. Reverend Sheldon Jackson founded the First Presbyterian Church in Golden in 1870, and two years later the red brick building was completed. When the Presbyterians outgrew it, the building was leased to the Unitarian Church until 1968 when the Foothills Art Center purchased it along with its manse. The old church complex, with an added second floor, is now alive with exhibits, lectures, classes, and concerts. A Victorian house next door, now known as Foothills II, was purchased in the 1980s.

Crook Museum

Crook Museum

Despite its title, the Crook Museum is not a collection of bank robbers' artifacts. Crook is a tiny community located on the north side of the Platte River between Julesburg and Sterling. It was named for Union general George Crook, well known as both an Indian fighter and Indian friend. His association with the area dates from 1875 when he took command of the Department of the Platte. He is better known for accepting Geronimo's surrender in Mexico in 1883.

This building was originally the First Presbyterian Church, built in 1910 in a somewhat altered form than it has today. In 1965, when the Presbyterians and Congregationalists combined to build a new church, the old structure was sold to Re-1 Valley School District for use as a band and music room. When a new school was built ten years later, the old building was deeded to the Town of Crook, and then donated to the Crook Historical Society. If the building should ever cease to be a museum, it will revert to the city.

The building looks quite new and contemporary at present with its simple, bold line and stark, unbroken walls; but its church origin is unmistakable.

Longmont—Polar Bear Gallery

In 1881 Bishop Spaulding laid the cornerstone for St. Stephen's Episcopal Church on Main Street in Longmont. Now this unaffected and appealing structure houses Barbara Stone's enchanting Polar Bear Gallery, but the building very nearly didn't make it to celebrate its centennial.

St. Stephen's was optimistically built for 150 worshipers, even though the congregation at the time consisted of only 35. But as Longmont grew, St. Stephen's membership increased. By 1970, 400 communicants were needing a bigger church at a more accommo-

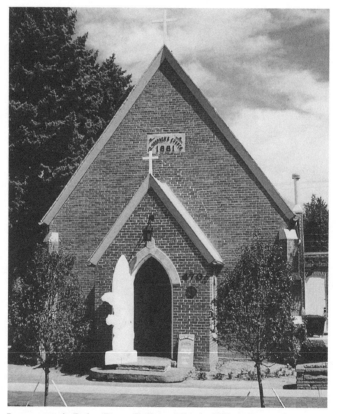

Longmont's Polar Bear Gallery. The building formerly wore a coat of white paint, and after St. Stephen's congregation left, it was known as "The Little White Church."

dating location. The church's property was sold to out-of-town businessmen, and its prime downtown real estate was targeted for commercial development.

The new owners intended to raze the historic church and its outbuildings. Fortunately the community rallied to save the church in a long and dramatic effort—the kind reenacted in hundreds of similar crises throughout the U.S. in recent decades. Five years and many fundraisers and heated meetings later, the campaign led by Ann Dine and Chris Linroth succeeded. Although adjacent buildings were torn down, the church was spared. This victory was truly a credit to Longmont's consciousness and to all the citizens who came to recognize the importance of saving this bit of their heritage. The building is now owned by the St. Vrain Historical Society and its existence seems secure.

San Juan Art Center in La Garita

La Garita - San Juan Art Center

The San Luis Valley settlement of La Garita (the lookout) was founded in 1852 on land that was once one of the largest Ute Indian camping grounds. By 1861 a small church was built, which unfortunately burned down. The La Garita Church, *La Capilla de San Juan Bautista* (Church of St. John the Baptist), was built in 1923. Since 1968 it has been the site of the San Juan Art Center, home to Artes del Valle, a Hispanic women's craft cooperative. Its distinctive five-pointed cross, visible for miles around, is said to be the only one of its kind in the United States.

Buena Vista Park Chapel. It was in the heyday of Buena Vista's mining days in the 1880s that pioneer Irishman, Thomas Starr, financed the construction of St. Rose of Lima Catholic Church (named for the first canonized saint in the Americas). When the little wooden church could no longer serve its growing parish, it was abandoned. The local fire department chose it to be burned down as practice in fire-fighting techniques. Just in the nick of time a restraining order was produced, and the structure was moved to its present location in a city park, where it languished another three years. In August 1972 the old church saw a new beginning. Finally rescued by citizens who cherished this relic of the old silver and gold mining heritage of the area, the beautifully restored building lives on as the Chamber of Commerce and Visitor Center in the now quiet mountain town of Buena Vista.

CONCLUSION

For pondering . . .

The trials and triumphs of Colorado's small-town and country churches are not unique. Few long-established churches lack dramatic, colorful, and even entertaining episodes in their histories. The examples presented in this collection illustrate something to keep in mind when admiring an old church building: there is a story to explain its appearance and its presence there on that particular site. Who were the people who built it, and why did they come? How did they raise the money? Who designed the building? Where did the stone come from, and how did it get to the site? Perhaps there once was a tower that toppled in some great prairie winds of 50 years ago, or it was hit by lightning, or never got built at all because the money was needed for something else. (Remember the copper cross on top of the Meeker church?) What kind of people were the individuals whose names are on memorial windows, and who made the windows? What is the legacy of the pastors who entered and exited the lives of this congregation and the community where they lived?

Unfortunately, the answers to these questions have often been lost, and with them our clues to understanding more completely that which remains. This is why recorded recollections by old-timers and written church histories are so important; they preserve the total heritage of a church and its relationship to the community. Just by their presence these structures are part of what we were and what we are, whether or not we have ever participated directly in the life of any church.

In July 1993 all that was left of the historic Lutheran Evangelical Hope Congregation Church near Bethune was a pile of rubble—the result of a tornado. Less than a year later, a spanking new brick church occupied the spot—accompanied by the one surviving tree. Thus the Hope Congregation justified its name, proving that even through natural disasters, there remains faith in high places.

BIBLIOGRAPHY

"1903-1978 Diamond Jubilee St. John's Ev. (sic) Lutheran Church, Windsor, Colorado."

"75th Anniversary Christ Episcopal Church, Castle Rock." 1982.

Abbott, Carl, Stephen J. Leonard, and David McComb. *Colorado: A History of the Centennial State.* Niwot: University Press of Colorado, 1982.

Adams, Rev. Anthony J. *Holy Trinity Church Centennial.* Trinidad: The Inkwell, 1985.

— "Ignatian Year Holy Trinity Parish, Trinidad, Colorado."

"A History of St. Stephen's." Compiled by Anne Mare Kimberling, 1990.

"A Vision of Faith: The 100 Year Journey of St. Mark's, Durango."

Anderson, Carleton. "The Mormons—100 Years in the San Luis Valley of Colorado." (Unpublished manuscript.)

Boulder Sunday Camera, "Austrian Empire Built Life, Church, Ranch on Dreams." May 31, 1987.

Bright, William. *Colorado Place Names.* Boulder: Johnson Books, 1993.

Bunker, Hazel. *A History of the Episcopal Parish of Saint Andrew at Cripple Creek in the Diocese of Colorado 1892-1958.* Copyright Hazel Bunker, 1960.

Carter, Carrol Joe. "Rocky Mountain Religion: A History of Sacred Heart Parish, Alamosa, CO." 1976.

Cassidy, Mary B. "St. Joseph's Church and Parish, Leadville."

"Centennial of St. Peter's Parish, Cripple Creek." 1992.

County Histories of Larimer, Fort Morgan, Las Animas, Sedgwick, and Lake Counties.

Crawford, Amanda Thornton. "Personal Reminescences (sic) of Calvary Episcopal Church of Golden."

Danhauer, Gary D. "Church History: First Baptist Church 1883-1984, Salida, Colorado."

Darley, George M. *Pioneering in the San Juan.* New York, Chicago, London: Fleming H. Revel, 1899. Community Presbyterian Church of Lake City copyright, second reprint edition, 1986.

Dawson, J. Frank. *Place Names in Colorado*. Denver: Golden Bell Press, 1954.

Donachy, Patrick L. *Echoes of Yesterday*. Trinidad: The Inkwell, 1983.

du Pont Beck, Allen. *The Episcopal Church in Colorado 1860-1963*. Denver: Big Mountain Press, 1963.

Dyer, J. L. *The Snowshoe Itinerant*. Cincinnati: Cranston & Stowe, 1890. Reprinted by Father Dyer Methodist Church, Breckenridge, 1975.

Edlund, Alvin, Jr. *100 Year History—First Christian Church (Disciples of Christ)*. Salida, Colorado.

English, Don. "The Early History of Fort Morgan."

Fiester, Mark. *Look for Me in Heaven*. Boulder: Pruett Publishing, 1980.

Flower, Judson H. Jr. "Mormon Colonization of the San Luis Valley, Colorado, 1878-1900." Masters thesis, Brigham Young University.

Foxhoven, Omer Vincent. "The City of God in the City of Gold." Copyright Foxhoven 1952.

Goodstein, Phil. *Exploring Jewish Colorado*. Denver: University of Denver Press, 1992.

Hanson, Eloise. "The Germans from Russia in Fort Morgan, From the Steppes to the Plains."

Henn, Roger. *In Journeyings Often—A Story of Ouray Told Through its First Church*. Ouray: First Presbyterian Church, 1993.

Hewitt, Rev. Neil C. *100 Years of Faith*. Leadville: 1979.

Hill, Nellie M. *High Country Parish, The History of Saint Patrick Catholic Church—Silverton, Colorado*. Saint Patrick's Catholic Church, Silverton: 1984.

"Historical Sketch of the Presbytery of Boulder, Colorado and Its Enrolled Churches from Organization 1883 to 1933."

"Johnson Memorial United Methodist Church, Historical Facts." Compiled by Nell H. Miller, 1994.

Kingdon, Esther Gunnison. "Ryssby, the First Swedish Settlement in Colorado."

Longmont Daily Times Call, May 14, 1981. "Little White Church."

— May 22, 1976. "Lyons United Methodist Church."

Marcy, Etta Marie. *The Brethren Church, Hygiene, Colorado*. Hygiene Cemetery Association, 4th printing, 1985.

Martin, Bernice. "People of the Book." 1956. Courtesy of Arnold Martin.

McCollum, Oscar Jr. *Marble—A Town Built on Dreams.* Denver: Sundance Books, Vol. I, 1992.

McTighe, James. *Roadside History of Colorado.* Boulder: Johnson Books, Revised Edition, 1989.

Morast, Ed. "History of La Foret." (unpublished manuscript 1957)

Morton, Jane. *Dyer, Dynamite & Dredges, The Story of a Breckenridge Church and a Colorado Pioneer.* Breckenridge: The Father Dyer United Methodist Church, 1990.

Murray, Andrew E. *The Skyline Synod: Presbyterianism in Colorado and Utah.* Denver: Golden Bell Press, 1971.

National Register of Historic Places nomination forms.

Nelson, David. "Ryssby: The Country Church."

— "Ryssby: A Swedish Settlement." *Colorado Magazine,* Vol. 54, No.2 Springs, 1977.

Outlander, Norma and Dorothy Kehrberger. "History of St. James Episcopal Church."

"Peaceful Valley Memorial Chapel, The Chapel That Love Built."

Pearring, John and Joanne. *The Walking Tour—An Historical Guide to Manitou Springs.* Manitou Springs: TextPros, 1983.

Ramey, Bertha. *History of Lyons United Methodist Church, Lyons, Colorado 1908-1973.*

"Revive 75, Parker United Methodist Church 1988."

Robertson, Josephine. "Guardian of the Valley." *Empire Magazine,* Sept. 10, 1978.

Schaefer, Jyle. *Faith to Move Mountains—A History of the Colorado District of Missouri Synod.* Denver: Colorado District Lutheran Church Missouri Synod, 1969.

Shawcroft, Betty and Robert Compton. "The Las Jara Stake of the Church of Jesus Christ of the Latter-day Saints." 1982.

Sheppard, Carl D. *Creator of the Santa Fe Style—Isaac Rapp, Architect.* University of New Mexico Press, in cooperation with the Historical Society of New Mexico.

Simmons, Virginia. *The San Luis Valley: Land of the 6-Armed Cross.* Boulder: Pruett Publishing, 1979.

Stegner, Wallace. *Where the Bluebird Sings.* New York: Random House, 1992.

"St. Mark's Presbyterian Church." Elbert County History.

Steward, Robert Laird, D. D. *Sheldon Jackson*. New York, Chicago, London: Fleming H. Revel, 1908.

Swartz, Dorothy. *History of St. Stephens Episcopal Church, Monte Vista*.

Taylor, Robert with Mildred Wesley. "History of the First Presbyterian Church of Crook."

Thompson, Thomas Gray, and Harold M. Parker, Jr. *The Oldest Church on the Western Slope—A History of the Presbyterian Church, Lake City, Colorado*. Boulder: Weekly Enterprises, 1976.

Ubbelohde, Carl, Maxine Benson, and Duane A. Smith. *A Colorado History*. Sixth edition. Boulder: Pruett Publishing, 1988.

Walters, Thomas. "T. MacLaren & Colorado Springs' North End." Denver. (unpublished manuscript)

Weaver, Frank. "The Old Stone Church." Assisted by the 85th Anniversary Committee (Lyons First Congregational), 1974."

Weigle, Marta. *The Penitentes of the Southwest*. Santa Fe: Ancient City Press, 1970.

"Zion's Lutheran 100 Year History." Trinidad: 1988.

INDEX